ENGLISH SKILLS
The Power for Professional Success

Editor
Masashi Nagai (Nagoya Institute of Technology)
Contributors
Akiyoshi Suzuki (Nagasaki University)
Teresa Kuwamura (Konan Women's University)
Kelly Quinn (Nagoya Institute of Technology)
Chikako Matsuura (Nagoya Institute of Technology)
Masashi Nagai (Nagoya Institute of Technology)

KAISEI

PREFACE

The present volume has grown out of our joint effort to investigate English skills as the driving force of professional success. The effort culminated in late December 2014, when the symposium on English skills and professional success took place at Nagoya Institute of Technology, Japan.

We hope that each article contributed here will help guide the ESP research in the right direction.

2015/03

Editor
Masashi Nagai (Nagoya Institute of Technology)
Contributors
Akiyoshi Suzuki (Nagasaki University)
Teresa Kuwamura (Konan Women's University)
Kelly Quinn (Nagoya Institute of Technology)
Chikako Matsuura (Nagoya Institute of Technology)
Masashi Nagai (Nagoya Institute of Technology)

CONTENTS

【論考 1】 ・・・・・・・・・・・・・・・・・1
英語力の数値管理とグローバル社会に対応する教育の齟齬—英米文学・世界文学の読みへの期待—
(鈴木章能)

【論考 2】 ・・・・・・・・・・・・・・・・・55
True or False? Business English and Internship in Japan　　　　　　(Teresa Kuwamura)

【論考 3】 ・・・・・・・・・・・・・・・・・81
Why E-learning materials fail　　(Kelly Quinn)

【論考 4】 ・・・・・・・・・・・・・・・・・99
Mastering English Skills for Professional Success: Reading Materials　　(Masashi Nagai)

【実践報告】 ・・・・・・・・・・・・・・114
名古屋工業大学海外交流の試み
—海外語学研修活動報告—　　(松浦千佳子)

英語力の数値管理と
グローバル社会に対応する教育の齟齬
―英米文学・世界文学の読みへの期待―

鈴木章能

1. はじめに

　文部科学省が 2003 年に「『英語が使える日本人』育成のための行動計画」を決め、「日本人全体として、英検、TOEFL、TOEIC 等客観的指標にもとづいて世界平均水準の英語力を目指す」とし、その具体的数値を示した。その直後の 2004 年、厚生労働省が「就職基礎能力」を、2 年後の 2006 年には経済産業省が「社会人基礎力」を公教育で身につけるべき能力として提言した。こうした決議や提言は、単に学習者の能力を向上させるという脱文脈的なものではなく、グローバル資本経済社会における個々の人生ならびに国益に資する対応という文脈において生まれたものである。日本の社会情勢としても、いわゆる大企業を中心に TOEIC スコアを採用の指標として学生に提出させるところが出てきた。文科省の決議は数値による英語の学習と教育の成果の出口管理に等しく、一方で企業側はその数値を入口管理として用いることから、学習者も教師も期待される英語力の「客観的指標」、とくに TOEIC における高得点を目指し、そうすることが学習者の将来に有益であるかのごとく、英語の授業を TOEIC 対策講座とすることも少なくない現状である。

　こうした英語学習・教育の状況について、これまでさまざまな議

論が展開されてきたが、本論では、議論の範囲を高等教育として、数値評価による英語学習・教育の出口管理とグローバル社会における人生や国益に資する教育は二重、三重の意味で矛盾し齟齬をきたしていることを指摘し、その克服の可能性を実社会の声の延長線上に見出し、提案してみたいと考える。

2. 目標管理型システムと英語教育

　最初に、現在の教育を取り巻く環境について確認しておこう。現在の教育を取り巻く環境とは、簡単に言えば、投資に対する成果を数値で測定評価し管理するという成果数値評価・管理システムである。これは個々の学生の成績はもちろん、授業評価や教員評価、大学といった組織への評価にも適用されている。TOEIC 等を客観的指標とみなし、英語教育ならびに学習の成果を数値評価・管理するという発想もまたこの文脈にあると考えらえる。

　さまざまな事柄が成果の数値評価によって管理されるようになった要因としては、「目標管理型システム」を核とする「ニュー・パブリック・マネジメント」の世界的蔓延が挙げられる。「ニュー・パブリック・マネジメント」とは「公的部門に民間企業の経営理論・手法を可能な限り導入しようという新しい公共経営理論」（大住 2002, 松下 2010: 10 の引用による）であり、「1980 年代の半ば以降、英国、ニュージーランドなどのアングロサクソン系諸国を中心に形成され、『民営化・規制緩和』が公共部門にも入ってきた 90 年代以降、世界的な潮流になっている」（松下 2010: 10）。このニュー・パブリック・マネジメントの核にあるのが「目標管理型システム」である。目標

管理とは、経営学者のピーター・ドラッカー（Peter Drucker）が1950年代半ばに提唱した「組織マネジメント手法であり、個々の担当者に自らの業務目標を設定させ、その進捗や実行を担当者に主体的に管理させる手法」（松下 2010: 10）である。昨今のシラバスはこの要領で書くことが義務づけられており、いわゆる学士力の重視やそれを具現化するディプロマポリシーと成果報告の義務化の背景もここにある[1]。

　目標管理型システムが学ぶ側のみならず教える側や運営する側をも取り巻くことになったのは、ドラッカーの理論が一人歩きした結果ではなく、グローバル経済に主な要因がある。その過程や日本の現状については、松下佳代（2010）が明快な議論を展開しているので、以下、松下に随時したがいつつ整理していくことにしたい。グローバル経済は「個人化」社会を到来させた。「個人化」社会とは、社会学者のウルリヒ・ベック（Ulrich Beck）がグローバル経済によって到来するであろうとかつて予想した社会のことで、「個々人が、家族の内外で市場に媒介された自分の生存保証と人生計画および人生編成の行為者となる」（ベック 1998, 松下 2010: 9 の引用による）社会のことである（松下 2010: 8-10）。そうした社会では、各々が資本主義の競争原理の中で自律的かつ主体的に生きていくための能力の教育が求められる。そこで日本では、後述するように「学歴＝能力」という等式が疑われるようになった昨今の事情とともに、「就職基礎能力」や「社会人基礎力」といった概念が生まれることになる。個人が自己の能力に拠って自律的かつ主体的にグローバル経済下の「個人化」社会を生きていけるようにすることが教育で目指されれ

ば、教育の過程の力点は当然のことながら入口ではなく出口に置かれ、出口において能力を客観的に可視化して評価することが能力の担保とみなされることになる。ここに教育と目標管理型システムとの接続点がある。日本の教育で英語力が重視され、かつ数値による成果の客観的評価測定が叫ばれるのも同じ原理である。グローバル経済社会が英語社会と等式で結ばれ、その社会の中で「個々人が、家族の内外で市場に媒介された」自分の生存保証や人生計画・編成を主体的に実現しなければならないとなれば、英語は人生を左右するに値する資本として重要性を帯びる。そうであればこそ、英語の授業は目標管理型システムの中で成果重視のスタイルを取らざるを得なくなり、能力の担保として成果を数値によって可視化する必要性が叫ばれることになる。英語力の客観的数値化こそが個々の学習者の将来の幸せに繋がるのであると。

　要するに、現在の日本の英語教育はグローバルな市場経済の中で幸せに生きていくための対応として、グローバルな市場経済を動かす民間企業の経営理論・手法のもとで展開されている。言い換えれば、学びと労働が同じ市場経済の原理とシステムの中に放り込まれているというわけだ。このことは、ここ数年の政策提言を見てみてもわかる。日本経営団体連盟は1999年に「エンプロイヤビリティ」、すなわち「雇用される能力」の確立を目指す政策提言をした。2004年には厚生労働省が「就職基礎能力」、2006年には経済産業省が「社会人基礎力」を提案した。いずれも実質的に産業界の好むスキル養成のための政策提案であり（松下 2010: 23-4）[2]、それゆえにスキル養成の成果測定もまたグローバル市場経済の経営理論・手法のもと

で数値によって評価されることになる。

3. 英語力を巡る客観的数値評価の限界

　ところが、英語力の客観的数値化は個々の学習者の将来の幸せに繋がるとは限らない。英語力の「客観的指標」と言う場合は一般に、選択肢を選ぶマークシート式テストが想定されている。論述の採点には主観が入りやすいため、マークシート式テストの採点結果が客観的指標になると考えられるためだ。その代表的なものがTOEICやTOEFLである。しかし、英語を使える能力というものは、そういった英語力の客観的数値指標によって可視化できるとは必ずしも言えない。これは、マークシート式テストがもつ性質上、必然的なことである。

　英語力をマークシート式テストで数値測定する場合は複数解答が可能な英文を読ませることはできない。文意が明確であり、英語という言語へのアクセスの仕方が正しければ、だれもが同じ意味として判断できる英文を問題文として読ませたり聞かせたりする。すなわち、マークシート式テストによる英語力の数値測定は、英語という言語へのアクセスの仕方が正しいかどうか、言い換えれば、正確な単語力や統語知識の有無を測っている。もちろん、そうした知識の測定にマークシート式テストは有効である。テストというものは、問いたい能力と問いが合致していればテストの意義が担保されるため、テストの形式それ自体を脱文脈的に否定することはできない。加えて、テストは学習者へのフィードバックの意味がある。また、テストに向けて学習者は高得点を目指して単語を暗記したり、文法

を理解したり、多くの文章を読んだり聞いたりして英文に慣れたりする。こうしたことが英語の習得に有効であることは、もちろん否定しない。ただし、ここで述べる英語の習得とテストの意義とは識字率の向上とその担保の意義である。後述するように、英語を現実の社会で（あるいは、後に展開する文脈に合わせて、グローバル経済社会で）使うこと、また使うことにおいて重要とされる機能リテラシーや知識の運用能力の向上のことではない。

　テストに代表される「発問」というものは大きく分けて三種類ある。英語の文章に直接示された内容を読み取らせる事実発問、英語の文章の情報をもとにそこには直接示されていない内容を推測させる推論発問、英語の文章に書かれた内容に対する読み手の考えや態度を答えさせる評価発問である（田中ほか 2011）。テストによる客観的数値評価は事実発問しか問えない。ほかの二種類の発問は複数回答を容認するからである。しかし、この、ほかの二種類の発問こそが、機能リテラシーや知識の活用能力の向上への道を開いている。

　たしかに、事実発問は読みの正確さをある程度まで計りつつ学習を促進するのには有効である。だが、読みの促進や動機づけ等の情意面で負の要素が出てくる（伊佐地 2012: 3）。また、事実発問は英文を正しく読むことが自己目的化する傾向にあるため、英文の内容を使って考えたり、なにかを感じたりという機会から学習者を遠ざける（鈴木 2014a）。ある一定の法則に基づいて並べられた記号を用いてなにかを考えたり、感じたり、行動に反映させたりするのが言語活動なのだから。こうしたことは「読む」ことばかりでなく、「聞く」ことについても同じである。そして、英語力の**客観的数値測定**

が学習や教育の効果を測るものとなるとき、いわゆる授業における頂上タスクは「高得点獲得」となり、英語の授業はおのずとそのための方法論の伝授となる。

　それでは英語が使えるようにはならない。英語が使えるとは、事実発問に正しい答えを導き出せることではなく、たとえば、英文を読んで喜怒哀楽を感じたり、新しい情報を得たり、批判的に考えたりすることであるし、それには、聖書をはじめとするさまざまな文化に根ざしたアレゴリーやメタファーが理解できることも重要である。また、書いたり話したりするときには、時と場合に合わせて丁寧な言葉を使ったり使わなかったりできるかどうかも重要であろう。そうしたことができなければ、たとえ一通の E メールでさえ、相手の本心や本当に伝えたいことは理解できないはずである。人間とつきあっている人が「わたしの彼は狼なんです」と言うのを耳にしたり、あるいは書いた文を読んだりしたとき、「斬新なご趣味ですね」と反応する者はいまい。「狼」がメタファーとして使われているためである。では、"If the salt loses its saltiness, how can it be made salty again?"と英語で書いてあったとき、文字通り「塩」の味について心配している意味の場合とそうでない場合があるのだが、後者の場合はどうするのか。

　いま書き並べたようなことは識字率が向上した後でできるようにすればよいのであるし、実際にそれは可能なのだという意見があるかもしれない[3]。だが、次項で見るように現実は異なる。グローバル経済社会であればこそ、現実は異なる。英語力の客観的数値測定による評価は、「エンプロイヤビリティ」や「就職基礎能力」や「社会

人基礎力」に関わる英語力の育成に寄与するように見えるかもしれないが、実際には両者の間に矛盾が生じているためである。その矛盾の一つとしてここで指摘したいのは内なる矛盾、すなわち、客観的数値測定による評価と、その評価の意義を支える目標管理型システムを核とする英語教育自体が矛盾しているという点である。しかも、二重、三重の意味で。

4. 一つ目の矛盾―客観的数値評価される英語力と現実の齟齬

まず一つ目の矛盾であるが、これは筆者がさまざまな職種に就く日本の人々に英語の必要性についてインタビューをした結果から導き出される。このインタビューは職種別の英語使用実態がわかる「E-Job 100」(http://e-job-100.sakura.ne.jp/modx/) という動画つきのホームページを作成するためにかつて行ったものであるが、詳細はインタビューの結果を含めて別のところで論じたことがある（鈴木 2014c, Suzuki 2014b）ので、ここでは概要を簡単に説明させていただく。筆者は、日本の労働人口の90%強が就いていると言われる約500職種の職業のうち約200職種について、英語の必要性／不要性について、その理由とともに尋ね、必要と言うのであれば、英語を用いる具体的な頻度やスキル内容、場面などについても尋ねたのであるが、その結果、程度や頻度の差こそあれ、2職種を除いて英語が必要であるという回答を得た。インタビューは、英語が明らかに必要であるとだれもが想像できる職種や大企業を除く職場を対象とした。その理由であるが、日本の多くの企業が中小企業であるという現実から、日本の大多数の人々にとって英語の必要性／不必

要性を説くには、英語が不要と一般に思われがちな職種の中小企業の実態を調査するのが適切であると考えたためでる。

　同インタビューで得られた結果は、現在ほとんどの職種で英語が必要となっており、その理由はグローバル社会にあるということである。起業家はもちろん、中小企業では社員のほとんどすべてが海外のクライアントと直接、コミュニケーションやネゴシエーションをしなければならないことも少なくない。加えて、社員教育などしている時間的・金銭的余裕はないため、即戦力を求めている。さらに、興味深かったのは、英語がただできるだけでは仕事にならないと回答したことだ。それらの回答をまとめてみると、英語で次の四つのことができる必要がある。

(1) 英文をじっくり読み、多元的な視点から解釈し、創造するあるいは既存の常識、あるいは信念体系を超える。
(2) 日常の外から、他国や日本の日常性に埋もれた人の在り方を眺められる（批判的視点や問題解決能力を含む）。
(3) 歴史的事実、感性を含む情緒、思考様式、習慣・慣習、伝統、法、文化など、日本とほかの地域を比較しながら、解釈の地平を広げられる力。
(4) 他者への共感や情緒を含めた豊かな人間性。（鈴木 2014c: 180, Suzuki 2014b: 91）

つまり、「エンプロイヤビリティ」や「就職基礎能力」、「社会人基礎力」に関わる英語力とは、ただ新聞や書類が読めたり、ただ会話が

できたりすることではない。ましてや事実発問に依拠する客観的数値指標のことでもない。自分の信念体系や理論的枠組みから一度はみ出して、他者や文章の「声」をじっくり聞き読み、感応し、共感し、地域に特有な文化、伝統、歴史、社会的現実、法、美的感覚をはじめとする感性等、言ってみれば、土地の「しがらみ」とともに他者の「声」を多元的に解釈したり、それをもとにして新たに創造したりすることで、英語ははじめて使える、言い換えれば、実用英語になるということである(鈴木 2014c: 180, Suzuki 2014b: 91-2)。上記した力は英語の識字率を上げたのち、卒業後に個々に学ばせればよいという意見は非現実的である。なぜなら、日本の多くの企業は中小企業であり、彼らが即戦力を求めているかぎり、英語教育の出口管理を数値評価に任せるだけでは現実と齟齬をきたすからである。逆に、後で学ばせればよいという主張が可能になるというのは、中小企業とは異なる雇用方法、すなわち即戦力を不要とする企業が日本の大方を占めるという前提に立っているということである。それならば、英語力を厳格な数値指標によって管理する必要はなくなる。なぜなら、英語力は卒業後すぐに必要でないということなのであるから。

　ところで、先に挙げた(1)から(4)の四点は文学の、あるいは文学を読む意義として、または、文学を読むことによってなし得ることとして、ハクスレーやエマソン、ロレンスをはじめ、昔から英米の文学者たちが述べてきたことである。鈴木(2014c)ならびに Suzuki (2014b)を手短にまとめて述べれば、(1)は広義の「文学を読むこと」であるとともに、イギリスの小説家オルダス・ハクスレー

(Aldous Huxley) が約 80 年前、情報量に重きを置くラピッド・リーディングに抗して、読みの質の重要性を主張したスロー・リーディングに相当する (Huxley 1933: 3)。あるいはクリスティーナ・ブランズ (Cristina Bruns 2011) が文学の読みの効用として指摘した、「他者」との出会いを通した「自己変革」の要素でもある。(2)はアメリカのラルフ・ウォルドー・エマソン (Ralph Waldo Emerson) が"Circles" (1841) というエッセイの中で文学の意義として述べている。日常の外から自分や社会や常識や当然と言われることをまなざす足場を付与することである。エマソン曰く「文学は我々のいまの円（日常）の外部にある点であり、そこからまた新たな円が描かれていく。文学は、自分のいまの生活を見渡す足場を与えてくれる。（中略）なにが真であるかという論拠や智慧は、百科事典にも形而上学の論文にも神学要論にもない。ソネットや劇にこそある」(Emerson 1990: 178)。(3)はイギリスの小説家 D.H.ロレンス (D. H. Lawrence) が「地霊」(Lawrence 1923/ 1964: 5-6) で述べた、ジョセフ・ショールズ (Joseph Shaules) の「深層文化」論を先取りするかのような、多元的な文学的まなざしに相当する。(4)は文学の伝統的な機能にあたる（鈴木 2014c: 180-3, Suzuki 2014b: 92-3）。TOEIC 等のテストにおける高得点を目指すだけの英語教育は日本の多くの人々にとっての「エンプロイヤビリティ」や「就職基礎能力」、「社会人基礎力」に関わる英語力を育むことが困難だということである。その能力を担保するには英米文学を読み多元的に解釈できるようにする必要があるということである（ただし、誤解を招かないようにここで断っておくが、言語学からのアプローチが不可能だと

筆者が考えているわけでない。文学と同じく言語学の知見からも可能であろうと考えてはいるが、筆者は文学のプロパーであり、言語学の深い知見に欠けるゆえ、ここでは文学からの知見となることをお断りしておく)。

　このことは、グローバル社会への対応を命題として提言された政策自体に裏づけを取ることができる。たとえば、クリントン政権において労働長官を務めた労働経済学者のロバート・ライシュ (Robert Reich) がグローバル経済社会への対応として提案した新たな三つの職業区分と最重視した能力を見てみよう。ライシュは職業を「『ルーティーン生産サービス』(モノ―金属、繊維、データ等―に対する単純生産)、『対人サービス』(人に対する感情労働を伴うサービス)、『シンボル分析的サービス』(データ、言語、音声、映像表象に対する問題発見、解決、戦略的媒介)」という新たな三つの範疇に分けた。そして、この中で「シンボル分析的サービス」の担い手の養成こそがグローバル社会において競争力を維持できるとした (松下 2010: 7-8)。シンボル分析とは「現実をいったん抽象イメージに単純化し、それを組み替え、巧みに表現、実験を繰り返し、多分野の専門家と意見交換をしたりして、最後には再びそれを現実に変換する」(ライシュ 1991, 松下 2010: 8 の引用による) ことである。これは文学の作りであると同時に文学を読むことそのもののことではないだろうか。そうした変換を英語で行える能力の育成が目指されるべきだというのであれば、英語圏文学を読むことがグローバル経済社会における英語教育に資するということになる[4]。

5. 二つ目の矛盾―PISA リテラシーとグローバル社会における教育

　現に、ライシュの述べるようなシンボル分析能力の育成を担保するために、いくつかのテストが作られている。その代表的なものが、シンボルの理解について正誤のみを判別するような従来のテストに代わって登場し昨今注目を集める PISA である。PISA は、DeSeCo (Definition and Selection of Competencies) のキー・コンピテンシーの中の「『道具を相互作用的に用いる』能力の一部を測定可能な程度にまで具体化したものである」(松下 2010: 23)。DeSeCo のキー・コンピテンシーについては後述することとするが、PISA が問うのは、いわゆる機能リテラシーのことである。機能リテラシーは、ウィリアム・グレイ (William Gray) が 1950 年代にユネスコ (UNESCO) の要請に応じて重視・提唱した能力である。樋口はグレイを借りて機能リテラシーを次のように説明する。

> 簡単なパラグラフの音読など初歩的なレベルでリテラシー教育を終えてしまうと、実際の生活場面でそれを生かすことができない。読むという行為には、音読ができるということのほかにも、黙読を通して意味内容を理解したり、自らの経験を豊かにしたりするといったことが含まれている。例えば、新聞やニュースレターから情報を得て好奇心を満たすということ、通知文や説明文を見て意味を理解した上で行動の変容をもたらすこと、さらには、表現の美しさを堪能し、楽しむために読むということ。このように、読むという行為にはさまざまな「機能」(役割) がある。(樋口 2010: 85)

グレイは、リテラシーが「日常生活での実用性に限定されるべきものでなく、政治にかかわる意志決定を自ら行ったり、社会活動に参加」したりすることをはじめ、「社会文化的かつ政治的な観点にも広げられるべきものであり、リテラシー習得が学習者の自立と社会参加に通じるものとなる」と考えた（樋口 2010: 85-6）。グレイの考えはその後、文化的リテラシーと批判的リテラシーの提唱に発展・継承されていく。E. D. ハーシュ（E. D. Hirsch Jr.）を主な提唱者とする文化的リテラシーは、「当該言語において読み書きのできる人々が暗黙のうちに共有している文化的な知識内容に光をあてる」（樋口 2010: 79-80）ことである。一方、パウロ・フレイレ（Paulo Freire）を主な提唱者とする批判的リテラシーとは、「『現実の対象化』、すなわち『世界にたいして距離を設定し、世界と自覚的に向かい合う』ことを通して、『既成の現実にたいする批判的な介入』を可能とする」（樋口 2010: 93）ことである。こうしてみると、グレイの主張は先にみた文学の機能（情緒的共感理解ほか）と一致するものであり、文化的リテラシーはロレンス、批判的リテラシーはエマソンが主張した文学の読みの効用と一致していることがわかる。そして、PISAの文章の冒頭には、グレイらの言葉が多々引用され、リテラシーの重要性が主張されている。

　留意すべきことは、そのような PISA がグローバル経済社会における企業の人材管理の評価方法の系譜にある点である。先に触れたように、PISA リテラシーは DeSeCo のキー・コンピテンシーの中の「『道具を相互作用的に用いる』能力の一部を測定可能な程度にまで

具体化したもの」である。この DeSeCo のいうコンピテンシー概念（そして「エンプロイヤビリティ」、「就職基礎能力」、「社会人基礎力」もまた）を辿っていくと、デイビッド・マクレランド（David McClelland）の Testing for competence rather than "intelligence" という論文に行き着く（松下 2010: 11）。マクレランドは、人材マネジメント会社のマクバー社の創始者の一人であるライル・M・スペンサー（Lyle M. Spenser）らと共同研究をし、スペンサーが構築したコンピテンシー・マネジメントの理論と方法の評価法「JCA」（戦略コンピテンシー評価法）を開発した。そして、この JCA が企業の人材管理に広く普及することとなる（松下 2010: 11-13）。ここで言われる「コンピテンシー」とは、「ある職務または状況において、基準にてらして効果的あるいは卓越した業績（performance）を生み出す原因となっている個人の規定的特徴」であると松下はスペンサーを借りて説明する。その特徴とは、「スキル（身体的・心理的課題を遂行する能力）、知識（特定の内容領域で個人が保持する情報）、自己概念（個人の態度、価値観、自己イメージ）、特性（身体的特徴、あるいは、さまざまな状況や情報に対する一貫した反応）、動機（個人が常に顧慮し願望する、行為を引き起こすもととなる要因）」と多岐に渡っている（松下 2010: 13）。すなわち、「従来、多くの組織が、表層の知識とスキルにもとづいて選考・採用を行い、採用後に、より基底的な動機や特性などを開発してきた」のに対し、「人間の深く柔らかな部分まで含む全体的な能力を評価し、労働力として動因・活用しよう」（松下 2010: 14）という考えをもとに新たなコンピテンシー概念が作られ、その評価法として JCA が開発されたのであった。

そして JCA は、「企業の人材管理の境界をこえて、高等教育の能力概念として援用」(松下 2010: 31) されることとなる[5]。この JCA のコンピテンシー概念と評価法に手を加えて教育の分野に登場したのが DeSeCo である。DeSeCo は、「エンプロイヤビリティにとって不可欠」であると見なされる「ジェネリック・スキル」(松下 2010: 19) と「その類縁概念(コンピテンシーなど)」がそれまで「混乱状態にあった」ところ、「理論的・概念的基礎の構築を目指し」(松下 2010: 19-20) て作られた。DeSeCo のコンピテンスの概念の構造は、「知識、スキルなどの認知的要素だけでなく、態度、感情、価値観と倫理、動機づけなど情意的・社会的要素も含んでいる」(松下 2010: 21) 点で先の JCA と似ているが、JCA のコンピテンシーが「内的な属性を直接、個人の能力の評価対象とする」のに対して、DeSeCo のコンピテンシーは「内的な属性を直接、そうした評価や教育の対象としているわけではない」(松下 2010: 21) 点で異なっている。また、DeSeCo のキー・コンピテンシーは、「個人の人生の成功(クオリティ・オブ・ライフ)」と「うまく機能する社会」という、個人と社会の両面から考えられたコンピテンシーである点にも特徴がある。それは「人生のさまざまな局面においてレリバンスをもち、すべての個人にとって重要とみなされるコンピテンシーである」(松下 2010: 21)。そのキー・コンピテンシーとして選択されたのが、「道具を相互作用的に用いる」、「異質な人々からなる集団で相互にかかりあう」、「自律的に行動する」という「三つのカテゴリー」である(松下 2010: 21)。これらは「個人の内的な属性と文脈との『相互作用』の産物」(松下 2010: 21) としてあり、常に三つのカテゴリーが組み

合わさって機能するものであると考えられる。すなわち、DeSeCoのキー・コンピテンシーとは「道具を介して対象世界と対話し、異質な他者とかかわりあい、自分をより大きな時空間の中に定位しながら人生の物語を編む能力」(松下 2010: 22)である。

　このDeSeCoのキー・コンピテンシーの中の「『道具を相互作用的に用いる』能力の一部を測定可能な程度にまで具体化した」のがPISAリテラシーである。すなわち、PISAリテラシーはグローバル経済社会において自律的に生きる力の有無を評価するものであり、そのPISAリテラシーがTOEIC等の数値指標では測り得ない、文学的読みを評価事項にしているというのであれば、TOEIC等の数値指標を英語教育の評価測定とすることは、「エンプロイヤビリティ」、「就職基礎能力」、「社会人基礎力」といった概念や定義が戦略的コンピテンシー評価の文脈にあるものであるからこそ、矛盾するのである。「エンプロイヤビリティ」、「就職基礎能力」、「社会人基礎力」の名のもとに英語教育を目標管理型システムの中で展開し、成果を数値で評価し、教育や学習の過程を管理するとき、その評価をTOEIC等の語学試験に託すことは、そもそも目標管理型システムの運用と矛盾をきたすことになる。

6. 将来の訓練可能性としての英語力の客観的数値指標

　以上、二点の矛盾について論じてみた。ここまで論じてきたところで、すでにお気づきとは思うが、新たな課題が見えている。そのことについては後で述べることとし、先になぜ上で見たような矛盾が起こっているのか考えてみたい。まず、筆者が経験したある出来

事について述べることから始めよう。それは職場における英語と大学の英語教育を巡る、あるシンポジウムでの出来事であった。そこには大学教員と「グローバル企業」と自社を紹介する一部上場の某大企業の人事係ならびに入社数年の若手社員が講師として登壇していた。質疑応答のとき、ある学生が「なぜいま、英語ではTOEICばかり重視されるのでしょうか。TOEICができたからといって英語ができるとは言えないし、英語で学ぶべきことはほかにもあるのではないのでしょうか」と、出席していた人事係に問うた。すると、その人事係は「たしかに、TOEICの得点と英語力がイコールであるとは限らないけれど、でも目に見えるものが必要でしょ」と答えた。その一方で、同人事係は、同社に入社する際、英語の能力はさほど重要ではなく、昇進のときにTOEICスコアが重視されるとも明言した。また、同社の若手社員は「入社して数年になるが海外とのメールのやり取りは、インターネット上の翻訳ソフトにかければ、なんとなく意味がわかるのでそれで十分です」とも言い切った。入社時の英語力は期待しないがTOEICのスコアは重視する、TOEICのスコアが一定以上のスコアであったから入社できたのであろう社員は英語が使えず、かつ「なんとなくわかるので十分」と言い切れるほど他者の発言に無関心である、それをグローバル企業と自社を紹介する人事係が問題と考えない等々、矛盾だらけではないだろうか。

　なぜ、この一部上場の大企業の人事係は、入社時の英語力はあまり必要ないと言うと同時にTOEICのスコアは目に見える能力の証拠として重要だといった矛盾した論理を持っているのであろうか。それは、まさに日本の大企業であるがゆえの論理と考える。田中

(2013)は、濱口桂一郎の日本型企業の整理を紹介して、「日本型雇用制度は長期雇用制度・年功賃金制度・企業別組合という三種の雇用制度に整理され、これらの結果、学校卒業者の一括採用→企業内訓練による人材育成→メンバーシップの形成という特徴が派生する」(189)のだと言う。だが、その結果として、「非正規労働者・女性労働者・中小企業労働者等の諸問題が必然的にわが国の特徴として発生している」と言う（田中　2013: 189）。ここで留意したい点は、日本型企業雇用制度があればこそ、中小企業労働の問題が発生するとしている点である。すなわち、大企業の論理と中小企業の論理は雇用制度の差異によって対立関係になっているという点である。先の田中の整理にしたがえば、一括採用とメンバーシップの形成は中小企業にも共通することから、対立関係を生じさせているものは企業内訓練、いわゆる社内教育であると言える。先に指摘した英語でできるべき四つの事柄は主に中小企業の声をまとめたものであった。彼らは即戦力を求めている。社内教育をする金と時間の余裕はないためであり、社員のほぼすべてが直接海外の人々とコミュニケーション、ネゴシエーションを行って仕事をしなければならないからこそ、先の四点を求めていた。と同時に、その四点はグローバル経済社会の教育がコンピテンシーとして重視するものでもあった。一方で、英語力について矛盾した論理をもっている大企業の人事係は社内教育があると述べていた。つまり、英語は社内教育や昇進の条件にすることで身につけていったらよいという論理である。

　大企業の社内教育のあり方は近年ずいぶん変わったという意見もある。日本の大企業の雇用制度を巡っては「かつては、仕事に必要

な特定の知識・スキルはOJT（On the Job Training）によって身につけられたのに対し」、それを「企業・従業員相互依存型」として今後は「従業員自律・企業支援型」に変化させることを重視しているという声もある（松下 2010: 24）。つまり、「企業によるOJTだけでなく、自助努力によるOJTを通じて、たえず自らの能力開発を行い、自己責任において雇用を確保していくことが、これからの労働者には求められる」（松下 2010: 24）ようになっているという。だが、社内教育の質が変わったところで、グローバル経済社会で即戦力を求める中小企業の論理からすれば、それは一種のモラトリアムである点で変わってはいない。そうであるからこそ、先の人事係の英語力を巡る論理が矛盾をきたしているのだ。

　即戦力を求める中小企業がTOEICのような客観的数値指標では測れない英語運用力を求めているのに対し、モラトリアムがあることにはいまも昔も変わりがない大企業がTOEICという英語の客観的数値指標を求めることにはいったいどのような背景があるのだろうか。日本の企業はかつて、「入社時に、新入社員が特定の知識やスキルを身につけていることを期待しているわけではなかった」。なぜなら「企業が日本的経営の中核的人材に求めるのは、フレキシビリティの発揮—仕事の範囲、仕事の量、ポスト、赴任地などの変動に積極的に適応できること—だったからである。そして、そのような企業においてフレキシビリティに富む人材と、学校においてどの科目でも総合的に成績が高く、性格的にも協調性・適応性に富む人材とは見事にマッチしていた。仕事に必要な特定の知識やスキルは、就職後のOJTで獲得させる。だから、入社してくる人材は、OJTに

よって仕事に必要な知識やスキルを身につけられるだけの『訓練可能性（trainability）』をもっていれば、それでよかった。学力＝学歴は、そうした訓練可能性の指標でもあった」（松下 2010: 25-26）。しかし、それが90年代半ばから異なってきた。「かつては学力が知識やスキルだけでなく、『動機（「やる気」など）』や『特性（「従順で素直な性格」や「前向きの性格」など）』をも示す指標として機能していた」のだが、「両者の間の相関関係が低下し、学力が動機や特性の指標としては十分機能しなくなった」ために、「学力とは別個に社会人基礎力を育成・評価する必要が出てきた」（松下 2010: 26）。そうであれば、大企業はかつての信仰をいまだ捨てていないのではないか。つまり、訓練可能性のある者を多く採用し、「やる気」や「前向きの姿勢」などを見るためにTOEICのスコアを求め、採用しているのではないのだろうか。実際、シンポジウムに登壇した大企業の若手社員は、某国立大学の大学院修士課程修了者であった。

　TOEICのスコアもまた訓練可能性としての能力の証なのであれば、TOEIC等による英語力の可視的証はグローバル人材という労働力育成に資する教育における客観的な能力指標として位置づけられているにも関わらず、実際の能力より可能性を求める姿勢によって形骸化される。学生の努力の証でもある「客観的数値評価」は、数値そのものより、その数値を獲得するまでの努力に力点が置かれ、能力より「努力できる」という可能性の評価にすり替えられる。こうしてみれば、英語力の客観的数値指標は、学生が大企業に就職しようと中小企業に就職しようと、英語が使える力を担保する指標にはならない。それにもかかわらず、英語力の客観的数値指標が叫ばれる

のは、グローバル企業というのはいまや企業の大小に関係ないにもかかわらず、大企業ばかりがグローバル企業だと勘違いされ、社内教育を行っている大企業的論理が日本で標準化してしまっているのはないのだろうか。

　そうした英語力の客観的数値指標の怪しさを、いまや学生は肌で感じているようだ。筆者が2014年度後期に勤務校の言語教育研究センターへ出講・担当した経済学部2年生の「総合英語Ⅲ」において、授業の最後にTOEIC等の数値評価テストと、筆者の授業を含めてこれまで受講した授業の体験から英語の授業について自分の思うところを自由に述べさせたのだが（2015年1月30日実施、回答数46）、46名中45名がTOEIC等の数値評価テストそのものを否定するつもりはないし、現在、社会から要求されるものであるため高スコアを目指さねばならないとは思っているものの、英語を学ぶことはTOEIC等の数値評価テストで高スコアを目指すことと同義ではないと記していた（1名はTOEICが社会の要請なら英語の授業ではTOEICだけをやればよいという回答であったが、諦めなのか賛意なのかは不明である）。加えて、TOEICの本はたくさん世の中で売られているのだから自分でやればよく、授業でわざわざやるものではない、授業では別のことを教えてほしいという声も多かった。また、TOEIC対策を内容とする英語の授業に対し、「大学入学試験対策となんら変わらない。勘弁してほしい」という回答が複数あった。大学入試のための英語の勉強が英語力に資さないという暴論も一般にあるが、この場合の英語力とは使えるという意味での英語力である。学生にとっては、TOEIC等による客観的数値指標を意識した英語学

習は、高得点・高偏差値という数値指標を目指す大学入試と同じであって、卒業後にすぐに英語を使うためのものではなく、また彼らの考える英語を使える力には資さず、TOEICであれ何であれ、客観的数値指標に管理された英語学習は英語を使う能力を身につけるためのものではないと考えているということだ。彼らは、英語やTOEICそのものを全否定するつもりはなく、TOEICだけが英語の学習や目標になってしまっていることに違和感を抱いているのであり、それより英語を使って他者との関係を生きるようにしたい、つまり、英語を言葉として使えるようになりたいと思っているのである。同様の思いは、先に述べたシンポジウムで質問した学生にもあるはずだ。彼の質問、すなわち、「なぜいま、英語ではTOEICばかり重視されるのでしょうか。TOEICができたからといって英語ができるとは言えないし、英語で学ぶべきことはほかにもあるのではないのでしょうか」という発言を確認すれば明らかなことである。

7. 「世界文学」への期待—グローバル社会で生きるためのリテラシーとグローバル社会の「ベル・ジャー」の可視化のために

　ここで先に残してきた新たな課題について指摘・考察しておきたい。先に日本の多くの人々が勤務する中小企業の声から、客観的数値指標に反映されるような英語の識字率だけでなく、英語圏文学の読みによって得られるような英語の運用能力が必要であることを指摘し、その能力こそがグローバル経済社会で生きるために重要な力であることをライシュが重視するシンボル分析から裏づけ、さらに、現在ではそうした能力を測るPISAやDeSeCoといったテストまで

あることを述べた。そして、それらのテストが、英語力の客観的数値指標を求める言説や「エンプロイヤビリティ」といった概念が依拠する企業の経営管理・手法と同じ系譜にある限り、単なる英語力の客観的数値指標だけでなく、英語圏文学の読みが英語教育において重要になると論じた。

　ここで留意すべきことは、PISA リテラシーが、たとえグレイたちのリテラシーの提唱に大きな影響を受けたものであるとしても、数値評価するために発案されたテストであればこそ、PISA リテラシーに寄与すると考えられる英語圏文学の読みもまた、数値化とともにグローバル経済社会を動かす企業の経営管理・手法に回収され得るものとなり、かつ数値指標化される可能性をもっているという点である。このとき考えるべきことは、文学の読みがリテラシー能力を高めるための読みとなり、能力の向上が自己目的化する可能性である。これは英語力向上の授業が客観的数値指標の名のもとに、実際の運用面を無視した単なる数値化への対策に堕すのと同じ論理である。こうしたことについて、益川 (2015) も次のように指摘する。

　　日本では、全国学力学習状況調査が毎年行われています。ほかにも国際学力到達度評価（PISA 調査）や、県単位で行われるテスト、学校単位や教室単位で単元ごとに実施されるテスト（自作や業者製作）もあるでしょう。
　　しかし同時に評価は、その仕組上（多肢選択問題や限られた記述問題では）、全ての能力を測定することはできません。そのため例えば、単元ごとに実施するテスト内容が「事実の暗記再

生と単純な読み書き計算の手続き」といった側面を重視していると、「テストの点数を向上させる」ための授業では学習者中心の授業と言いつつも直接的な指導を、授業時間外ではドリル練習やテスト対策学習を中心に取り組むようになるでしょう。これでは本末転倒で「確かな学力の育成」ではありません。

　また、全国学力学習状況調査やPISA調査などのプログラムでは、教育政策やその地域の行政責任者の説明責任が強調されるため、それに応えなければならない教師たちは苦悩を感じてしまうことも多々あります。評価は、本来目指している子どもたち一人ひとりの学びの向上とは関係のない「順位付け」や「選別」に使われてしまうことが多いのも現状です。

益川は初等教育や中等教育を前提に指摘しているが、その指摘は高等教育にも言えることである[6]。

　数値による英語力の出口管理を否定するはずの文学の読みがPISAの数値指標のもとで実践されれば、文学の読みもまた単に資本主義経済における労働力をいかに効率よく育成・選抜するかという論理に巻き込まれてしまう恐れがある。だが、文学の読みをそのように悲観視する必要もないと考える。文学の読みはPISAリテラシーの数値評価もまた越えていくと考える。第一、リテラシーの一つである「批判的リテラシー」とは「『現実の対象化』、すなわち『世界にたいして距離を設定し、世界と自覚的に向かい合う』ことを通して、『既成の現実にたいする批判的な介入』を可能とする」ことだった。先に見たように、エマソンは「文学は我々のいまの円（日常）

の外部にある点であり、そこからまた新たな円が描かれていく。文学は、自分のいまの生活を見渡す足場を与えてくれる。(中略)なにが真であるかという論拠や智慧は、百科事典にも形而上学の論文にも神学要論にもない。ソネットや劇にこそある」と述べた。英語圏文学の読みは、英語によるリテラシー能力とともに、そうした能力を要求する生活を俯瞰する眼力を与えてくれる。

　たとえば、トム・ルッツ（Lutz 2006）が指摘するように、アメリカ文学の特徴の一つとして労働主義へのアンチテーゼを挙げることができる。労働それ自体へのアンチテーゼではない。なぜなら、作家たちは執筆という労働に精を出しているのであるから。ましてや勤労でもない。田中（2013）が指摘するように、勤労という言葉は日本の社会制度で用いられる場合、歴史的に天皇のための労働になるからである（田中 2013: 130-50）。そうではなく、社会一般を覆っている労働概念ならびに労働という制度に我と我が身を預けることに対するアンチテーゼである。したがって、アメリカ文学は働くということ—もっと言えば、アメリカ的労働であり、現代のアメリカ文学であればグローバル経済社会のシステムに身を預けること—について距離をもって眺める足場を与えてくれる。アメリカの小説家シルヴィア・プラス（Sylvia Plath）は代表作『ベル・ジャー』（*Bell jar*）で、自分が覆われているものの透明であるゆえに普段は気づかず、覆われているゆえに息苦しく、覆われているゆえに望むものに自由に手を伸ばしても、その手を遮る透明なガラスの容器「ベル・ジャー」を可視化した。読者に自分を覆う「ベル・ジャー」の存在に目を向けさせ、目の前の世界をそのように見えさせている「ベル・

ジャー」について考える機会を与えた。英語の識字率、リテラシー、学士力、「エンプロイヤビリティ」などは現実の問題として避けては通れないのかもしれない。しかし、そうした要求ならびにそうしたことを要求する世界を当然と見て我と我が身を預けるのではなく、ましてや息苦しさや不自由さを感じるのであれば、自分を覆う「ベル・ジャー」について考えてみればよい。グローバル経済社会、資本主義、それに関するさまざまな管理・手法やシステムという「ベル・ジャー」に覆われている自分の姿が見えてくるであろう。常に日常の外に立ち、日常を眺めることで、いまここにある世界があるシステムの侵食を受けて成り立っていること、自分がシステムの中で生きているに過ぎないこと、そしてそうであれば、いましなければならないと要求されていることなど真理でも何でもなく、さまざまな言説が我々の生きているこのグローバル化した資本主義という制度から立ち現れてきていることを看破し、生きるということの意味を考えつつ、他者をそして自分をミスリードしないことが重要である。文学はその意味で、数値化社会の中に生きつつ数値化社会に距離を置き、資本主義社会に生きながら資本主義社会から距離を置き、生きるということの意義や人生のあり方を再確認させてくれるきっかけとなろう。

　「ベル・ジャー」をさらにはっきり可視化したければ、資本主義が世界に蔓延したいまだからこそ、資本主義に相対する概念、すなわちマルクス主義のまなざしとともに世界を考えることも重要であろう。英米文学をマルクス主義的に読むということである。もっと簡単な方法としては、現在のグローバル経済社会で起こっている事

象について、共産国の文学から考えることもいいであろう。「〇ヶ年計画」といった計画のもとにあらゆることが進められ、その成果を数値化し判断するという現在の日本社会で広く行われている公共管理の手法は、そもそも共産主義国家の計画経済の方法ではなかったのか。マルクスは一つの国の内部で発展段階説を説き主張したために、イマニュエル・ウォーラーステイン (Immanuel Wallerstein) らの登場もあって、一時はその論理が疑問視されたが、地球上のほとんどが資本主義に覆われ、資本主義の外部が消えつつあるいま、マルクスの予言は無視できない。先の計画経済のような公共管理は、もしかすると地球が何の暴力革命も経ず、すでに共産主義への途上に着いたことを示す現象なのかもしれない。その真偽のほどはともかくとして、数値化社会と言えば、ロシアのエヴゲーニイ・ザミャーチン (Yevgeny Zamyatin) は1920年代、ロシアの行く末を『我ら』(*We*) というディストピア小説に描いた。ディストピア小説では、ユートピア小説で描かれる世界とは反対の世界が描かれる。国家あるいは集団が徹底的な管理システム、監視システムを用い、人びとの衣食住のあらゆる範囲に管理・監視システムが及んだ絶望的な世界が描かれる。ザミャーチンの描く世界は、共産主義の行く末であるものの、現在の教育の行く末であるとも読める。すなわち、あらゆることが数値化され、数値化されることを重視する世界の行く末である。ちなみに今日、英語圏以外の文学を英語で、すなわち翻訳で読む意義や効用が「世界文学」の理論によって担保されている (Damrosch 2003, 2009)。世界ではいま、さまざまな地域の文学を英語で読み、我々を覆う「ベル・ジャー」をクロス・カルチュラ

ルに、クロス・ポリティカルに可視化し考えていく方向にある。

あるいは、文学は次のような視線も作ってくれる。人生や社会はすべての物事が合理的に進めばうまくいくのかもしれない。そうした社会や人生に、文学は合理的でないもの、すなわち「他者」を侵入させる。突然「他者」が侵入しないような人生や社会などないであろう。文学は、すべての物事が合理的に進んでいく中に立ち現れる「他者」をどう受け止めるのか、逆に「合理的」であることがどのようなことなのか考えさせてくれる[7]。

こうした視線を持つべきは、学生もそうだが、まずもって教師なのではないのだろうか。教師が我々を覆っている「ベル・ジャー」を可視化できなければ、当然と思われている物事の人為性や政治性、不自然さを看破できず、真理でもないことを真理だと言って強制し（とはいえ、アンケートにあるように、学生は肌で感じて気づくものなのだが）、常に学生を右往左往させるか、ミスリードしていく危険がある。すなわち、教師が英語の識字率向上や客観的数値指標の向上に向けた工夫だけを知っているのでは不十分ということである。まずもって教師が文学の素養を（そして言語学の素養も）、あるいは現代風に言うのであれば、リテラシーを身につけておくべきであると考える。

8. 授業案

最後に、ここで論じてきたことを実践する授業案を記して本論を閉じよう。先のアンケートを行った授業のことである。もちろん、これが完成形とは考えていない。改良の余地は大いにある。なお、

筆者が担当したクラスは習熟度別に分けられた中位の下位クラスであったが、英語の識字率の向上に関しては系統的な知識を一から教授する必要はなく、学習者の多くが躓く箇所のみを解説していく形式が可能なクラスであったことを先に述べておく。なお、英会話については初回の授業の時点でできる者は一人もいなかった。また、学習のモチベーションであるが、当初はそれほど高くなかったものの、授業を通じて次第に改善していった。初回の授業が始まる前にモチベーションの低さを想定し、授業の内容を通じて改善していく工夫を用意しておいたのであるが、一定の効果があったものと思われる。授業の内容については後述する。

　さて、筆者が勤務する大学の教養英語の授業でもG-TELPが客観的数値指標として義務づけられているのだが、筆者の授業ではその数値を高めることを目標にはしなかった。筆者の授業の概要は以下の通りである。シラバスから転記する。

　　入学以来高めてきた英語力をさらに高める。具体的には、日本の労働人口の95％が就く約500職種のうち約200職種の調査からわかった英語の運用能力の習得を行うことである。それは、他者への共感理解に基づいた正確な英語理解と英語運用能力である。このことから「文学的」な英文の読みにビジネスシーンを組み合わせた授業を展開する。将来のキャリア選択、専門の授業、将来の学習計画にも結びつけられるようにする。

つまり、先に述べた英語でできるようになってほしい四つの事柄と

英語の識字率をともに向上させることを目標とする授業を行った。また、日本の学生は他国に比べて教室内で孤独感や無能感といった社会的排除の感情を強くもっていること（鈴木 2014a）、現代社会が資本主義の競争原理で動いていること、ならびにグローバル経済社会は排除の構造をもっている（Young 1999）ことを憂慮して、言語によって自己も他者も幸福感に満ち、より良い人間関係を構築できる英語力を習得するという目標も据えた。つまるところ、英語の授業が相手にするのは「客観的数値」ではなく、人間それ自体であるという立ち位置である。もちろん、識字率としての英語力の向上を無視したわけではない。識字率が限りなくゼロに近ければ、言語で他者との関係に生きることはできない。

そこで到達目標として次の三つを掲げた。

1. 4技能を網羅して、英語が正確に運用できる。
2. 英語がただ使えるだけでなく、他者への共感的理解から適切な英語の理解や表現ができる。
3. 文化的差異から他者や自己を考えた英語の運用ができる。

これらを実現するための形式的方法は以下の通りである。

1. 授業を重ねるごとに英文のグレードを少しずつ上げていく。
2. 各職種調査から英語使用の実態を動画やテキストで確認できる E-Job 100 のサイトを利用して、求められる英語力を確認する。E-learning も併用する。

3. 4技能を網羅した英語力を高めていく。そのため、毎回頂上タスクを設定し、それに基づいた英文の読解やアクティビティ等を4技能満遍なく行う。グループに分けた英語による発信も行う。
4. 常に他者のことを考えた英語運用力を意識し、実社会で他者との関係を英語で生きている力を身につけていく。
5. 以上のことから、「文学的」英語理解とビジネスシーンでの英語理解を交互に、且つ融合しながら英語運用を練習する。

以上を実現するための毎回の授業内容は次のとおりである。

1. グローバリズムと日本と英語について。なぜ「文学的」英語力なのか。
2. 英語によるさまざまな紹介 1 (Ice-breaking、パラグラフ構成)
3. 英語によるさまざまな紹介 2 (英会話力向上の方法と練習)
4. "The gift of the magi"を読む（共感理解、言語による良好な人間関係、社会的排除の軽減）
5. "The gift of the magi"を読む（会話による良好な人間関係、社会的排除の感覚の軽減）
6. "The marriage of convenience"を読む（自己の内側から感じ考える）
7. "The marriage of convenience"を読む（文化的差異へのまなざし、多元的解釈、イデオロギー、共感的理解、批判的志向。

ディスカッション、発表）

8. ビジネスシーン（対人関係、ディスカッション、意見を傾聴する・読む、課題解決）
9. ロールプレイング（文化的差異を英語で体験する）
10. ポライトネス（文化的差異と英語の表現）
11. ポライトネス（ビジネスシーンに広げて）
12. ケーススタディ 1（グローバル・ストラテジー、4P 理論の理解、文化的差異と他者への共感理解を踏まえた英語での仕事）
13. G-TELP
14. ケーススタディ 2（発表。総合的タスク）。
15. エマソン、ハクスレーらのエッセイを読む（新しい視線の構築とまとめ）。

　毎回の授業内容に一つ一つ触れながら、授業全体の流れを説明しておく。初回は授業全体の説明、ならびに授業内容について本論で述べた日本社会と英語の必要性の現状について説明を行った。また、先に触れた筆者の「E-Job 100」を紹介し、随時見るように述べた。
　2 回目は、教室内でのより良い人間関係を構築するために ice-breaking を行った（同アクティビティは英語で行った）。まず、学生にビンゴのマスを九つ作らせる。クラスのほかの学生に氏名を尋ね、三つの質問をし、回答を書き留める。これが一マスに書き入れる情報である。それを 9 人分行わせる。これらはすべて英語で行わせる。その後、ビンゴの要領で 3 名を選ばせ、その 3 名について、

あらかじめ用意した物事を紹介する文章の型を使って英作文をさせた。言い換えれば、パラグラフライティングの方法を教えた。

　3 回目の授業では、2 回目の授業で書いた英文をすべて暗記させ、暗記した文章を用いてさまざまなものを紹介させることで、英語が話せるようになること、また話すことを体験させ、かつ英会話の習得の方法を教えた[8]。このとき、英会話を中心に、英語の識字率向上のための基本として次のようなことを学生に話した。すなわち、英会話の習得はピアノのレッスンと同じであり、週に一度教室に出かけていって指導者の言うとおりにしているだけではピアノの腕など上がらないように、英会話も週 1 度の授業だけでできるようにはならない、残りの六日間はピアノを毎日弾くのと同様、家で毎日練習してほしい、と。要するに、対日本語において日々口にする英語の量を増やすことの重要性を述べた。それとともに、英会話の習得は日々の英語の使用量をどれだけ多くするかということが重要であり、その点ではアメリカやイギリスにいようと日本にいようと同じことであるゆえ、知性よりむしろ心（意識と意志）が重要な鍵となるとも付言しておいた。もちろん、ピアノは日本の家庭でも日々練習できるが、外国語としての英語は使用する場を見つけねばならないゆえ、どのように日々練習するのか、そのアイデアを学生にいくつも紹介した[9]。以降、解説した英会話の習得の方法にしたがって練習してもらった成果を学生が体感できるようにするべく、毎回の授業の最初の時間を使って、"What did you do in the last weekend?" をテーマとする英会話を学生同士で行ってもらった。はじめは 3 分程度、以下回を追うごとに時間を延ばしていき、最大 20 分程度英語だけで

会話ができるようになった。

　毎回の授業内容に戻ろう。4回目と5回目の授業では、O. ヘンリー（O. Henry）の「賢者の贈り物」（"The gift of the magi"）をテクストとし（リライト版）、人間の思いやりを描いた文章をじっくり味わってもらったのち、クラス内の複数の人々の長所を三つ見つけ、"I like you because ..."といった文を用いて互いに英語で褒め合ってもらった[10]。これにはいくつかの狙いがあった。まず、脳科学者のダマシオ（Damasio 2005）にしたがえば、何かを感じない限り、人は何も考えようとしないし考えられないゆえ、次回以降の授業内容を考えて、学習者の情緒に訴えるテクストを使用した。また、先に触れたように、日本の学生は学校や教室で居場所のなさや無能感を感じる傾向にあり、このことが教室での活発な学びやアクティビティを阻害していると考えられるため[11]、学生たちの孤独感や排除の感覚を軽減し、彼らが互いに受容されているという感覚を持てるようにしようとも考えた。これは後の協働に向けた仕掛けの要素ももっている。

　6回目と7回目の授業では、5回目の授業で長所の指摘とともに褒めてもらった経験をもとにウィリアム・サマーセット・モーム（William Somerset Maugham）の「政略結婚」（"The marriage of convenience"）を読ませ（リライト版）て「幸せとは期待しないことである」というテーゼを個々の内側から考えさせ、英語で意見を述べてもらった[12]。すなわち、体で感じたばかりの幸福感を客観視させるということである。また、テクストが多文化的内容になっているため、多元的な視点に立ったテクストの解釈や「幸せ」につい

ての考察ができることも目指した。

　6回目の授業でテクストを読んでもらい、英語やテクストの背景等について解説を行ったのち、7回目の授業でテクストならびに「幸せ」について多元的解釈をしてもらった。具体的な方法であるが、まず「幸せ」について、結婚について（本テクストの「幸せ」は結婚を文脈としているため）、また人間関係について、サマセット・モームの時代のイギリス、ならびにテクストに出てくる複数の国や地域の時代、政治、文化、宗教、社会的現実など多元的な文脈から考えさせる。それをもとにテクストの内容について多元的に解釈させる。その後、「幸せ」の意味を巡る差異と共通点を踏まえて、文化的社会的構築物としての人間と、類としての人間にとっての「幸せ」の意味、ならびに「幸せとは期待しないことである」というテーゼについて意見を述べてもらう[13]。

　8回目の授業では、前回の授業を受け、「幸せ」な人間関係が仕事でももっとも重要であることを理解してもらうのと同時に、職場において異なるジェンダーや文化に属する人々の間で人間関係が崩れたときの英語の会話文を読ませ、どこに問題があるのか、会話文を分析し考察してもらった[14]。ここで学生に留意させたかったことは、文化的差異に目を向けない他者の無理解と英語におけるポライトネス表現の失敗である。前者については6、7回目の授業で行ったことに即して考えさせ、後者については、テクストから一歩引いてテクストを批判的に読み分析すれば、適切な言葉や文法が選択できるようになるため、より良い言語習得が可能になるというウォレス（Wallace 2003）、コッツ（Cots 2006）、ジャンクス（Janks 2008）

らの指摘も踏まえ、またそれ以前の授業の内容とも関連させ、相手の良いところを見つけて言葉にしても、英語の表現が不適切であれば誤解を招くことを理解してもらい、適切な表現ならびにその選択について学んでもらった。

そこで、9回目の授業では、まず文化的差異によるコミュニケーションの成否を体験してもらうため、英語の会話文に続けて「次の一言」を選択し、その選択によっていくつもの場面に分かれて話が進んでいくロールプレイ式の英文を読ませた [15]。親切心から生まれる他者への言葉や行動が文化的な誤解のために勘違いされること、言ってみれば、やさしさのすれ違いの悲劇が体験できるようになっている。この英文を読むことで、他者の立場に立ったコミュニケーションの重要性を認識してもらった。

続いて10回目の授業では英語の表現が英語圏文化と密接な関係をもっていることを解説し、ポライトネスに焦点を当てた英語表現の用い方を教えた。具体的には謝罪と感謝の言葉である。加えて、「もし自分であったらどう言ってほしいか」をまず考えさせ、それでは「相手もそう言ってほしいであろう」という思考を介在させて謝罪や感謝の適切な表現を選ばせることで他者を尊重したコミュニケーションの力を育もうともした。

11回目の授業では、10回目で行った謝罪と感謝以外の場面と表現に範囲を広げ、日常生活とビジネスの両場面において、作文や会話を行った。はじめは紙面で、のちに会話の中に適切なポライトネス表現を取り入れて練習を行った。

12回目は、多元的解釈と他者の尊重を仕事の内容に広げるため、

グローバル・ストラテジーを使ったケーススタディについて英文テクストを用いて理解してもらった。グローバル・ストラテジーとは、企業が異なる国や地域で販売を促進するために、販売先の文化、慣習、思惟様式、法、社会的現実等、多元的な解釈をもとに、自国と同じ製品／異なる製品を、自国と同じ製品名・広告で売るか売らないか、あるいは新製品を作って販売するのか、五つの組み合わせをローカルとグローバルの視点から決定する戦略である。五つの組み合わせについて、その例を英文で読ませ、インドで日本製の洗濯機を、またアメリカと中国で日本製の自転車を販売する際のストラテジー決定を考えてもらった[16]。

13回目の授業ではG-TELPの試験を行い、14回目の授業では12回目で学んだグローバル・ストラテジーを用いて、インドでの洗濯機販売とアメリカ・中国での自転車販売のケーススタディについて英文で簡潔に述べさせた。

15回目の授業では、ここでも紹介したエマソンらの英文を用いて授業で行ってきた内容を総括するとともに、マルクス主義の要諦を簡単に説明し、我々がいま生きている世界の基底について説明した。

全体的なことについて付言しておく。授業で扱った内容のうち時間の関係から十分な解説ができなかったものについては参考文献を紹介し、学生に随時参照してもうようにした。また、授業中は、必要に応じて語用論や文法の説明（ただし、訳読からの脱出を目指した意味の範疇化や認知文法による説明）を行ったり、作文では学生が書いた英文を座席の列ごとに回覧して学生たちみんなで英語の正確さや内容についてコメントを書き合ったのち、筆者が一つ一つを

添削して戻すという「協働+フィードバック」の方法を用いたりしたほか、さまざまな方法で英語力の向上を試みた[17]。

さて、この授業の成果であるが、識字率については義務づけられている G-TELP (Level 3)と筆者が作成した期末試験（期末試験は主に語用や認知文法の理解を問うた）で、リテラシーについては筆者が作成した期末試験で確認した。また期末試験では授業評価を自由書式の形式で行った。

まず G-TELP の結果から見てみる。勤務校の 1、2 年生は 1 年生の後期、2 年生の前期、2 年生の後期の各セミスター13 回目の授業時に G-TELP を受験している。ここでは 2 年生前期の結果と後期の結果を比較し、平均点の変化を分析することとする。受講生 47 名のうち、2 年生後期の G-TELP を受験した学生は 46 名であった。このうち、2 年生前期の G-TELP 受験者は 43 名であり、前期と後期の成績の進捗度を見るため、両方の G-TELP を受験した 43 名の学生について調査することとした。以下は総合点の記述統計量（300 点満点）である。

表1. 2年生前期と後期における総合点の記述統計量

	N	平均	標準偏差	最大値	中央値	最小値
前期	43	183.6047	12.0636	202	185	163
後期	43	193.2093	29.0037	254	195	134

次に、総合点の平均点の変化を検証する。検証は、筆者の勤務校に

おける G-TELP の結果分析を行っている小笠原（2013）に従い、2年生の前期と後期の平均点の差に対して、対応のあるペアによる t 検定（一対の標本による平均の検定ツール）を行った。帰無仮説を「前期試験の平均点と後期試験の平均点には有意差は無い」とし、$p<.05$ 両側検定によって分析した。分析結果は表2のとおりである。

表2. G-TELP Level 3 総合点（TOTAL） 前期後期の比較

	前期	後期	差
平均	183.6047	193.2093	9.6046
分散	145.5305	841.2171	
観測数	43	43	
ピアソン相関	0.315648		
仮説平均との差異	0		
自由度	42		
T	−2.27583		
P(T<=t) 片側	0.01401		
t 境界値 片側	1.681952	P(T<=t) 両側＜0.05 だから棄却	
P(T<=t) 両側	0.02802		
t 境界値 両側	2.018082	→平均点の差に有意な差がある。	

表2の分析の結果、有意な平均点の変化（平均点の上昇）を確認す

ることができた。

　加えて、上記結果を TOEIC 換算してみる。これも勤務校に適した小笠原（2013）の数式「TOEIC スコア＝2.308×G-TELP スコア－13.39（R^2＝.568）」に従う[18]。それによれば、筆者が担当した学生の2年生前期の TOEIC スコア平均は 410.369、後期の TOEIC スコア平均は 432.537 となり、22 点以上の上昇があったと言える。

　一方、期末試験で問うた語用や認知文法の理解は、知識の確認が目的であったこともあり、正答率の平均は 80％ という結果となった。

　また、期末試験で問うたリテラシーについてであるが、問としたのは現在のリーバイスの状況が書かれた英文を読ませ、同社のジーンズをイギリスで販売する際のストラテジー決定を英文で報告書として書かせるというものである。多元的な視点から状況を分析できているか、多元的な視点からストラテジーを選んでいるか、ストラテジー決定の根拠が的確なものであるか、報告書は適切なパラグラフ構造をもっているか、ポライトネスを含めた適切な表現で書かれているかなど、授業で行った内容が総合的に英文に反映されているかどうか確認した。結果は、46 名の受験者のうち 45 名が合格点を得た。

　最後に、期末試験のときに自由書式で行った授業評価についてであるが、回答者 46 名全員から授業に満足しているという回答を得た。その理由であるが、英語を実際に運用できるようにすること、運用するときにはどのようなことに気をつけ、それをどのようにして学び、どのように練習するのか、現実の場面で具体的に練習できたこと、しかも他者を受け入れ共感理解し合いながら練習できたことに

対し、高い評価をもらった。改善点を指摘する記述はなかった。なお、受講生たちはそれまで英会話だけ、TOEIC対策だけという授業ばかりを受けてきたらしく、筆者の行ったような授業を受けるのがはじめてのようだった。補足であるが、「賢者の贈り物」を読ませた授業終了後、学生たちが筆者のもとを訪れて、このCDはないかと尋ねてきた。理由を尋ねてみれば、「賢者の贈り物」にとても感銘を受けたとのことで、こうした名作を読むだけなく、聞くことでリスニング力も高めたいと申し出てきたのであった。「賢者の贈り物」を大学2年生まで読んだことがないという事実に正直驚いたが、それはともかく、彼らの反応は、文学作品がいかに効果的な教材であるのか、また文学作品がいかに人の情緒に訴え行動を喚起する大きな力をもっているか、確認できる事例である。

　以上、英語の識字率と運用力を向上し、グローバル社会で生きる力（距離を置く力も含めて）を培い、さらに他者を受容・共感理解・尊重し、他者の立場に立ってコミュニケーションがとれる人格を養う具体的な授業実践について概略した。改善点はいくつもあると考えるが、少なくとも客観的数値指標や識字率の向上だけを目指す英語の授業よりは、英語力の向上に資すると考える。

9. おわりに

　本論では、現在の英語教育、とくに客観的数値指標による出口管理とグローバル経済社会における教育の齟齬・矛盾について指摘するとともに、英米文学ならびに世界文学の読みに矛盾を解決する可能性を見た。英語力の客観的数値指標による出口管理を、現在の教

育を取り巻く環境の文脈で捉え、数値指標が本当に有効であるのかどうか、社会で求めてられている英語力についてプラグマティズムの立場から考察した結果、同英語力の育成は英語圏文学の読みが有効であり、したがって客観的数値指標とグローバル経済社会における英語力の育成には溝があることがわかった。現に文学の読みは、グローバル経済社会で最重要とみなされる力と重なり、またそうした力の有無を評価するPISA等のテストも生まれている。TOEIC等による客観的数値指標が声高に叫ばれるのは、現在文科省や教育が民間企業の経営管理・手法によってグローバル経済社会への対応を展開しているためではあるが、実際にそうした要求の声を支えているのは、少数派である日本型大企業の論理、すなわち客観的数値指標を実際の英語力として捉えず、将来の訓練可能性を示す努力値として扱う姿勢にあると考えられる。一方で、多数派の中小企業はTOEIC等のテストで測れない、文学の読みによって培われる英語力を即戦力として求めているのであるから、TOEIC等を英語力の客観的数値指標として英語教育・学習の出口管理に用いるのは、ほとんど意味のないことである。とはいえ、PISAの登場で文学の読みが数値化されれば、文学の読みもまたグローバル経済社会における効率的人材選抜に資するだけのものになる懸念も出てくる。だが、文学の読みは常に日常の外から日常をまなざす足場を作ってくれるゆえ、PISAというテストの数値指標に回収されることからも、グローバル経済社会の諸システムに回収されることからも逃れ、そうしたことから常に一歩距離を置くリテラシーをも身につけられる。以上の議論を踏まえて具体的な授業案を最後に示した。繰り返しになるが、

この授業案は一案であり完成形ではない。しかしながら、多面的な成果が出たことは確かである。改良を加えたものを別の機会に提案したいと考えている。

*本研究はJSPS科研費25370672の助成を受けたものである。また本論は、名古屋工業大学FD研究会「仕事力と英語力の交差」(於　名古屋工業大学、2014年12月19日)における口頭発表「いま英語教育に求められているもの—プラグマティズムから考える英語教育—」の原稿に加筆修正を加えたものである。

注
[1] ドラッカーの目標管理型システムは大学のみならず高等学校等にも及んでいる。数値指標の例としては大学入学者数が挙げられる。目標管理型システムを核とする高等学校の教育現場の状況については、日永(2014)を参照。また、このことによる高等学校の教育現場の混乱については、植田・小野川(2014)を参照。
[2] これは大学のみならず、高等学校に対しても言えることである。児美川(2014)、林(2014)、植田・小野川(2014)を参考。
[3] もちろん、大学生の英語力そのものが低下しているからこそ、数値化による厳格な出口管理を行うようになったことはわかるし、英語力がなければ、ポライトネスも何も理解できないという意見もわかるが、しかし、いまや英語力とともにここに並べたことを身につけていく英語の授業は中学校でも、また中学校との連携を考えた小学

校での英語の授業でも行われつつある。長崎大学教育学部附属小学校・長崎大学教育学部附属中学校編（2015a）135-46、（2015b）186-207を参照。

[4] 文学を読むことの効用や他国の文学を読むことの原理的考察については鈴木（2014a, 2014b, 2014c）、Suzuki（2014a, 2014b, 2014c）を参照。また、読書案内を含んでいる日本で容易に入手できるものとして大浦（2013）を挙げておく。なお、筆者は文学だけが読めればよいと述べるつもりはない。外山（2007）がかつて「アルファ読み」と「ベータ読み」の両方の読みが大切であると指摘したことに同意する。ここでは、「アルファ読み」ばかりが目立つ英語教育において「ベータ読み」の重要性をプラグマティズムの観点から論じている。そして、外山もまた「ベータ読み」には文学を読むことが重要であると結論づけている。

[5] ただし、アメリカではすでにコンピテンシー・マネージメントのブームは沈静化している。松下（2010）は、アメリカでは90年代にコンピテンシー・マネージメントの限界を指摘する調査や論考が次々と出されてブームが沈静化した一方で、日本では2000年代半ばになって高等教育分野で経営学のコンピテンシー概念が脚光を浴びるようになっており、皮肉なことであると言う（松下 2010: 41）。ちなみ、安冨（2014）は、現在教育にも導入されている公共経営理論の核たるドラッカーの理論をそのまま日本で用いても文化的基盤が違いすぎるために機能しないと指摘している。

[6] PISAには日本の地域的問題もある。リテラシーが日本に移入されたとき、本来は統一された能力と位置づけられたものが「PISA型

学力」と「PISA 型読解力」と「活用力」といった形で教育現場に浸透している（松下 2010: 23）。すなわち、「キー・コンピテンシーのうちの指標化された一部だけがある種の屈折を経て移入されている」（松下 2010: 23）という問題がある。

[7] 文学を英語教育のみならず、ほかの教科教育にも連動させようとする動きが世界的に出ている。たとえば、古典文学を社会に応用する Hestia のプロジェクトがある。このプロジェクトを巡り、筆者も文学、英語教育、地理学、歴史学を繋ぐ原理的研究をバーミンガム大学でのシンポジウム（2014 年 4 月 30 日）にて発表した（発表の要旨は Suzuki 2014a を参照）。筆者の考える原理を具体的な授業に反映させる方法ならびにその意義として、濱浦（2014）の「メンタルマップ」を応用し、学習者の世界認知を「いま・ここ」から広げることが考えられる。また、文学を英語教育で用いて英語によるリテラシー能力や思考力を高める具体的な指針と方法としては、土肥（2014）の三種類の社会問題と授業でのアプローチの整理が参考になる。土肥によれば、社会問題は(1)「社会に実在する客観的な状態（ないし欠損状態）」、(2)「行為や政策、制度などをめぐる、価値観の異なる個人・集団による選択・判断の相違や衝突によって形成されたもの」、(3)「社会問題を個人・集団の間のコミュニケーションを通して構成・再構成される、集団的なカテゴリーや定義づけの産物」という三つの立場から捉えられる。そして、それぞれ(1)は「構造規定としての社会問題」、(2)は「価値葛藤としての社会問題」、(3)は「定義闘争としての社会問題」と言い表される。授業ではこれらについて異なるアプローチが用いられる。(1)を扱う授業は「問題を

生じさせる因果・機能・要素につい考察」、(2)を扱う授業は「複数存在する判断の構造を明らかにする」、(3)を扱う授業は「これまで実際あった過程で、今後も継続したり、類似したことが起きるような過程を把握する」。このように具体的に整理された三種類の社会問題と各アプローチは文学テクストで扱われる内容ならびにテクストへのアプローチと重なっている。それゆえ、土肥が整理した各社会問題と各々に結ばれた各アプローチを、文学テクストを媒介にして英語教育で展開すれば、英語によるリテラシー能力や思考力を高める具体的な指針と方法になると考える。このことについては稿を改める。ただし、文学の読みは指針や方法によって限定されなければならないということなどまったくないが。

[8] 筆者の経験において役に立ったもののうち、学生にとっても気軽に使えると思われる方法について紹介した。紹介したのはインプットについてもアウトプットについても理論ではなく具体的な方法や工夫である。たとえば、アウトプットに関しては、体育会のクラブに所属し、海外留学ができる金も時間もなかった松本道弘（1987）の、日本を英語圏諸国に見立てて英語を話し、英会話を習得するという発想と方法は、似た境遇にあった学生時代の筆者にとって非常に役立った。また、インプットに関しては、日ごろ英文の読みに時間を割いてばかりいるように思われる、戦前戦後を代表する英米文学者たちが英会話をどのように習得したのか、こちらも参考になった（大橋ほか 1979）。

[9] 注8を参照。

[10] 用いたテクストは、加藤がリライトしたもの（加藤 2010）である。

なお、紙媒体とインターネット等の電子媒体の読みの差異を巡る Ulin（2010）の指摘を受けて、読ませるものは必ず紙媒体とした。

[11] 詳細は鈴木（2014a）を参照。

[12] 用いたテクストは、加藤がリライトしたもの（加藤 2010）である。

[13] この具体的な方法ならびに理論については、Suzuki（2013, 2014c）、鈴木（2014b, in print）を参照。

[14] 用いたテクストは、藤井ほか（2002）である。

[15] 9回目から11回目の授業で用いた英文は、広東外語外貿大学の李筱菊名誉教授が編集した教材の一部を用いた。この教材の特長や李名誉教授の言語哲学については、桑村（2009a, 2009b）を参照のこと。

[16] 用いたテクスト、ならびにグローバル・ストラテジーによるケーススタディを用いた英語の授業の意義と効果については、桑村（2013）を参照。

[17] なお、学生たちにはさらに、リスニングと単語力増強のためのEラーニングが言語教育研究センターからあらかじめ課されていることも申し添えておく。ただし、筆者が確認した学生たちの学習履歴、ならびに学習したことを見せかけるソフトの存在から、彼らがそうしたEラーニング教材にどこまで真剣に向かったのか判然としないと正直申し上げるべきであり、その意味で、彼らが「Eラーニングを日々行った」とここには書けないと考え、注で断ることとした。

[18] 小笠原（2013）は過去のテストデータから、単回帰分析によってテスト間の相関を0.75、決定係数を$R^2 = .568$としている（小笠原

2013：52)。

Bibliography

伊佐地恒久（2012）「教材案」、生き方が見えてくる高校英語授業改革プロジェクト『知的プロセスを大切にした高校英語授業のモデルの開発　授業プラン集』、

3-9.(http://www.ecrproject.com/index.php?plugin=attach&refer=Senior%20High%20School%20English%20Classroom%20Reform%20Project&openfile=20120810.pdf) 2013年11月18日アクセス

植田建男・小野川禎彦（2014）「高校教育の実践課題と希望—『教育再生』をどう読み解くか」、小池由美子編『新しい高校教育をつくる—高校生のためにできること』新日本出版社、241-65

大浦康介（2013）『フィクション論への誘い—文学・歴史・遊び・人間』世界思想社

大橋健三郎ほか（1979）「私の英語学習法」、朱牟田夏雄ほか『現代の英語教育—12　英語研究法』研究社出版、158-83

小笠原真司（2013）「長崎大学学生の英語力伸張に関する研究　—1年間のG-TELPのデータ　から—」、『長崎大学言語教育研究センター紀要』1、47-66

加藤和美（2012）「The Gift of the Magi」、「The Marriage of Convenience 」、生き方が見えてくる高校英語授業改革プロジェクト『知的プロセスを大切にした高校英語授業のモデルの開発　授業プラン集』、10-29.

(http://www.ecrproject.com/index.php?plugin=attach&refer=Senior%20High%20School%20English%20Classroom%20Reform%20Project&openfile=20120810.pdf) 2013年11月18日アクセス

桑村テレサ（2009a）「外国語教育におけるC.ロジャーズの『学生中心教育』の理論的展開と実践」（学位論文）奈良女子大学

桑村テレサ（2009b）「中国に見るヒューマニスティック英語教育―李筱菊のCLT(Communication Language Teaching)について―」、『英語英文学論叢片平』44号、107-123

桑村テレサ（2013）「『適応戦略』を用いた英語教育―文化的多様性へのまなざしをもった思考力と英語力のために―」LEORNIAN 17号、33-42

児美川孝一郎（2014）「権利としてのキャリア教育」、小池由美子編『新しい高校教育をつくる―高校生のためにできること』新日本出版社、87-102

鈴木章能（2014a）「『生きる喜び』を見い出す英語の授業―英語教育改革一案 あれかこれかを超えて―」、『英語英文学論叢片平』49号、183-196

鈴木章能（2014b）「ポスト理論と世界文学の時代―日本的まなざしから英語圏文学を読むことを巡って―」、鈴木章能編『East-west studies of American literature as world literature & essays―あるアメリカ文学者の系譜―』、2-45

鈴木章能（2014c）「中庸の英語教育―仕事現場の声、世界文学、教育学の視座から―」、柳瀬陽介、組田幸一郎、奥住桂編『英語教師は楽しい―迷い始めたあなたのための教師の語り』ひつじ書房、

鈴木章能（in print）「国民文学、世界映画（ワールドシネマ）としての『ラスト、コーション』―世界文学の視点から考える多国籍世界映画試論―」、片平会編『片平50周年記念論文集―英語英米文学研究―』金星堂

田中萬年（2013）『「職業教育」はなぜ根づかないのか―憲法・教育法のなかの職業・労働疎外』明石書店

田中武夫・島田勝正・紺渡弘幸（2011）『推論発問を取り入れた英語リーディング指導―深い読みを促す英語授業―』三省堂

土肥大次郎（2014）「社会問題に対する思考力育成を重視した中学校社会科授業の研究」、長崎大学教育学部教職実践研究委員会編『教育実践教育フォーラム in 長崎大学』長崎大学教育学部教職実践研究委員会、37

外山滋比古（2007）『「読み」の整理学』ちくま文庫

長崎大学教育学部附属小学校・長崎大学教育学部附属中学校編（2015a）『平成26年度教育研究発表会学習指導案集』長崎大学教育学部附属小学校・長崎大学教育学部附属中学校

長崎大学教育学部附属小学校・長崎大学教育学部附属中学校編（2015b）『平成26年度教育研究発表会研究紀要』長崎大学教育学部附属小学校・長崎大学教育学部附属中学校

濱浦翔（2014）「地域認識を育む教育の研究―メンタルマップ活用を通して―」、長崎大学教育学部教職実践研究委員会編『教育実践教育フォーラム in 長崎大学』長崎大学教育学部教職実践研究委員会、26

林萬太郎（2014）「高校生に必要な職業労働教育とは何か」、小池由美子編『新しい高校教育をつくる―高校生のためにできること』新日本出版社、103-22

樋口とみ子（2010）「リテラシー概念の展開―機能的リテラシーと批判的リテラシー」、松下佳代編著『＜新しい能力＞は教育を変えるか―学力・リテラシー・コンペテンシー』ミネルヴァ書房、80-107

日永龍彦（2014）「学校評価と開かれた学校づくり」、小池由美子編『新しい高校教育をつくる―高校生のためにできること』新日本出版社、195-215

藤井正嗣・リチャード・シーハン（2002）『英語で学ぶ MBA ベーシックス』日本放送出版協会

ベック、U．（1998）『危険社会―新しい近代への道―』東廉・伊藤美登里訳、法政大学出版社

益川弘如（2015）「テストによって評価することの学力への影響」、平成 26 年度長崎大学教育学部附属小・中学校教育研究発表会」配布資料

松下佳代（2010）「＜新しい能力＞概念と教育」、松下佳代編著『＜新しい能力＞は教育を変えるか―学力・リテラシー・コンペテンシー』ミネルヴァ書房、1-42

松本道弘（1987）『松本流英語道のすすめ』KK ベストセラーズ

文部科学省（2003）「『英語が使える日本人』の育成のための行動計画」

http://www.mext.go.jp/b_menu/shingi/chukyo/chukyo3/015/siryo/04042301/011.htm、2015 年 2 月 5 日アクセス

安冨歩 (2014)『ドラッカーと論語』東洋経済新報社

Bruns, C. V. (2011) *Why literature?: The value of literary reading and what it means for teaching.* New York: Continuum.

Cots, J. (2006) "Teaching 'with an attitude': Critical discourse analysis in EFL teaching." ELT journal 60/4, 336-45.

Damasio, A. R. (2005) *Descartes' error: Emotion, reason, and the human brain.* New York: Penguin Books. (Rep.)

Damrosch, D. (2003) *What is world literature?* Princeton: Princeton University Press.

Damrosch, D. (ed.) (2009) *Teaching world literature.* New York: Modern Language Association of America.

Emerson, R. W. (1990) Circles. *Essays: first and second series.* New York: The Library of America, 173-84.

Huxley, A. (1933) *Texts and pretexts: An anthology with commentaries.* New York: Harper and Brothers.

Janks, H. (2008) "Teaching language and power." S. May and N. Homberger (eds.) *Encyclopedia of language and education* 1, New York: Springer Verlag, 183-94.

Lawrence, D. H. (1923/1964) *Studies in classic American literature.* London: Heinemann.

Lutz, T. (2006) *Doing nothing: A history of loafers, loungers, slackers, and bums in America.* New York: Farrar, Straus and Giroux.

Suzuki, A. (2013) Cross-cultural reading of doll-love novels in Japan and the West. *Journal of East-West thought*, Fall Issue, 3(3), 107-126.

Suzuki, A. (2014a) Topographic unconsciousness. *Hestia* (http://hestia.open.ac.uk/topographic-unconsciousness-2/). Accessed on February 5, 2015.

Suzuki, A. (2014b) Need for Anglophone literature for Japanese students in a globalized society: Developing a resilient life. *Lit Matters*, Summer 2014 1(1), 86-106.

Suzuki, A. (2014c) How should we read literature from a certain area from the viewpoints of other language-speaking areas? *The IAFOR journal of literature and librarianship*, Winter 2014 3(1), 9-39.

Ulin, D. L. (2010) *The lost art of reading: Why books matter in a distracted time*. Seattle: Sasquatch Books.

Wallace, C. (2003) *Critical reading in language education*. London: Routledge.

Young J. (1999) *The exclusive society: Social exclusion, crime and difference in late modernity*. New York: Sage.

True or False?
Business English and Internship in Japan

Teresa Kuwamura

1. Introduction

Today's Japan, educational organizations are making efforts to train people to be able to independently and actively live and work in a global society.[1] Many business organizations in Japan have plans to develop and expand their business abroad such as setting up new branches to ride on the wave of globalization. As a way to prepare for this, traditional English education has shifted its focus to offer Business English class and seek internship in the foreign countries. Author has received education from five countries and acquired work related experiences in four countries. Based on the personal experience, author feels both Business English education and foreign internship projects in Japan are not practical and far away from the real world. American psychologist, educator, and the founder of student-centered education Car Rogers pointed out that a person can only significantly learn something in his or her real world (1951, 1969, 1982, and 1994). In this paper, author has drawn a comparison between Business English classes and internships between Japan and other countries by pointing out the differences and providing suggests for possible improvement, which may bring positive impact to English education in universities in Japan.

2. Author's Experience and the Facts

Author's first internship experience was in the U.S. after she was enrolled in the MBA program. Almost all the students in this program took part in internship. Most of the students took a break from the school to join their full time internship programs during the summer quarter which is from the middle of May to the end of August. The crowded campus became empty during that time. Author started her internship job at Washington State China Relations Council as an assistant to the Chinese affairs for the state government. On the first day, after a very brief greeting and introduction, author was told to prepare and send out claims to Chinese central government with cover letters. All employees and interns were busy dashing between their assignments in the office area. No formal instruction was given to the author on how to perform each task. In fact, nobody had time to. There was no Chinese word processor software installed on the computer for typing the cover letter. After consulting with the supervisor, author was told to write the letter by hand with neat handwriting and find a better solution later independently. After finishing writing the cover letter and preparing the document, author found envelops at the corner and put all the letters in the envelopes and then wrote addresses on them. However, since there was no stamp at office, author decided to wait for the supervisor who was in a meeting.

When the supervisor saw all envelops were still on the desk after finishing his meeting, he was upset. He and the author had a serious conversation. He helped the author to understand American office rules. Intern is treated as the staff when he or she starts an internship. Every staff member must individually complete his or her own task on time including overcoming difficulties and finding creative solutions for any problem encountered. The staff needs to complete task on time without excessive instructions from the supervisor. It is a common sense in America. By his advice, author downloaded and installed a free Chinese words processor the first time in the office and established a communication channel between the state government office and the Chinese central government office by letters, e-mails, telephone conferences, and Faxes. Since then, author has learned to work independently with any job including assisting the claim between Boeing corp. in the U. S. and China. After graduating from the MBA program, author was offered the same job as she interned based on the positive feedbacks from the supervisor.

The most important lesson author has learned was the sense of ownership for a job. Critical thinking, quick decision, effective communication, professional style, and independence are all the skills author learned from the internship.

3. University Education and Internship in Other Countries

Based on personal experience from the author in the U.S. and Singapore, during the four years study at universities and colleges, besides the regular classes on campus, students take part in internships in society. Internships are known for giving students the opportunity to apply their knowledge they learned in the classroom to the real world environments and also providing opportunities to build up skills which help the students to perform better at their future jobs.

In the business society, people need both interpersonal and leadership abilities. Many university educational curriculums are good at teaching students analytical skills but not practical experiences. In the U. S. and Singapore, university programs strongly encourage students to join internships. By effective internships, students can increase their skills and make themselves more valuable in the job market. Students who participate in internships tend to perform much better than students who graduate from schools without going through any internship. After completing their internships, most of the graduates can learn the skills necessary to succeed in their future careers. Those are evidences that education only at school are not enough to allow graduates to perform at a higher level.

American and Singaporean university curriculums often try hard to impress their perspective students by advertising how many internship opportunities their students have and how much grant they receive from the private industry and government. Universities in America and Singapore have their own career development offices. After students enroll a school, they are encouraged to start their internship early. In American universities, internship programs are flexible and diverse. In general, there are two types of internship. One is incorporated with the school curriculum. When a student completes this type of internship and receives a satisfactory result, the internship is counted as certain number of credit towards the total number of credits needed to graduate. Another type does not count as a credit but for students' own future career benefit. If qualified, students can participate this type of internship anytime during the school year with the school's support. Internship can also be either part time or fulltime. Students usually take part time internship and take class from the school at the same time. For fulltime internship programs, students often take them during their vacation time particularly in the summer.

Most of the college students in America and Singapore start to look for their first internships before the first summer quarter after enrolling into their schools. The main information resource is the career development office on campus. Faculties and student advisors provide full support to the students on seeking a suitable program. Resources and guidance are always available to help students in their internship search. Most of the students can manage their own internship opportunities with the support of the advisors. Direct approach and proposition to the employer would be the normal way. A proactive and enthusiastic students always find there are more opportunities than the others. Other students gain chances from media and their personal or family connections.

American universities usually help their students to find an intern opportunity by following several steps. First, students are asked to think ahead because internship application procedures and deadlines vary based on the employer, location, and popularity. Students are encouraged to make full use of the internship to synthesize classroom theory and develop personal skill and genuine career-related work experience. Students seek out real world assignments that can expand their learning experience into the areas that are not available in the classroom. They look for the programs that help themselves to become expertise at the workplaces and integrate what they have learned by focusing on output, results, and what can be achieved if they participate. Second, students make sure their goals of internship are to sharpen their skills and gain experience by working in a real-world work environment. It is wise to utilize a variety of methods in seeking an internship and to pursue opportunities with persistence and confidence. The quality of students' experience, the development skills, and their motivation and enthusiasm are ultimately the most important aspects. Third, students are asked to think about their career choices and link their future careers with a goal of internship programs. The questions of which students should think regarding their career choices are

- Why do I want an internship?

- What do I want to learn from an internship?
- What sort of company or organization would enable me to learn I needed?
- Where do I want the internship geographically?
- How much time do I want to spend at an internship?

Those are common questions that help American university students to organize their ideas before they start applying their internship programs.

In the U.S. and Singapore, applying for an internship program is similar to apply for a real job. Student needs to prepare his or her resume with a cover letter is often necessary. The advisors at the carrier development office take the responsibility of helping students to prepare their resumes and supporting documents. To gain an internship is the first challenge from the real world for many student. In many cases, it is very competitive for an intern vacancy because the internship interview processing is almost the same as a real job interview. It is a cutthroat competition among applicants particularly for a good internship opportunity. Sometimes a student has to fight with hundreds of competitors for a position. Some universities offer special courses for internship interview training. Even with the advice from the student advisors, a student must go through necessary processes by themselves for gaining an intern chance.

An employee in the U.S. or Singapore has the duty to complete his or her own job assignments since the first employment day by all means. An employer looks for the new graduate who has good talent such as high motivation, leadership, good oral communication skills, experience, independency, good interpersonal skills, and so on. It is the duty of a supervisor to help an employee to get familiar with the job functions. However, the only way an employee can really learn is by performing the job. The common sense to a student who has not only completed his or her education systematically but also gained training experiences is that he or she ought to contribute to employer from the first employment day. Unlike the Japanese system, a new employee starts to contribute to the employer from day one even during the training period in the U.S. With this type of cultural value, society requires graduates to have enough experience and adaptability to a new job. Common skills required are the abilities to solve problems independently, critical thinking, and computer skills. An intern is treated similarly to an employee. An internship period is essentially a training for students to get used to a job and perform reasonably well. Graduates can work as an experienced employee from the first working day after becoming a fulltime employee. An intern has his or her own responsibilities to the jobs and the organizations. He or she has to report the progress to the supervisor. An intern must learn and find a way to complete his or her own job individually as well as cooperate with the others. In the U.S. and Singapore, a job duty of students who participates in internship programs could be as tough as the one given to a new employees. Internship also allows students to learn about time management, discipline, and effective communication skills. In the business world, critical thinking skills are particularly important. Without an internship, it would be very difficult for a graduate to perform well initially. Graduates must be able to make quick decisions based on their experience. Internship teaches students how to excel in the large organization and industry. After students complete their internship programs, they have learned to solve problems and communicate effectively. In addition, it is also important to know how to use different types of media and technologies. Students develop their abilities in the area of oral communication, team work, and leadership skills. With those skills, graduates are competent to pursue their future careers.

  Because many American employers feel not all college

graduates have enough practical experience to excel in the real world, internships have become more important than ever before. After completing their internships, students not only have gained experiences from their jobs but also shown their capabilities in their resumes that are what employers are looking for. It is also advantageous when students are seeking for the new jobs. Through an intern program, many interns obtain the same jobs after their graduation. It is beneficial to both the employers and students because no additional training needed from the employer side and no need to look for a job from the student side. It is one of the most important methods that the college graduates go through an internship program and receive a job offer.

4. University Education and Incompetent Internship in Japan

In this chapter, author describes Japanese college internships based on her experiences in setting up oversea internship programs as part of the new curriculum at her school, Konan Women's University.

In order to well prepare students to thrive in the new era of globalization, author's school has decided to expand the educational curriculum and establish a new program, English and Business, a few years ago. This program integrates a variety of learning experiences so that our graduates are capable and confident to function in today's multi-cultural, multi-ethnical, local, and global business environment. Unlike many other universities in Japan, author's school has planned to provide our students with a practical training opportunity via the job placement and extra-curricular activities. To provide a stage to the students, author's school has determined to set up a project where students can improve their English and have an opportunity to open the door to the real business world. Author and her school have researched most of the existing internship programs in Japan and felt very frustrated as the results were far away from students' real needs.

There are several types of programs called internship provided to the university students in Japan. The typical ones as an example is sponsored by the warfare group where students can obtain training abroad. The destinations include China, Korea, and Indonesia. All the juniors at Japanese colleges and in the universities can apply by submitting an essay and pass the interview. The warfare group offers financial aid by paying half of the expenses for the trip to the qualified participants. In addition, the group sponsors the full cost for the best candidate. It is a good program for the students. However, it is not the true internship program our students needed after reviewing the details. During the four day trip, students are scheduled to listen to an introductory presentation given by the warfare group branch office, visit the group organizations, sightsee cities, and participate a dinner party. Students do not have a chance to practice English nor complete any work related assignment.

 To match our students' interest, author and her school also performed research on the fashion industry internship opportunities in Japan. A famous Japanese fashion chain store offers an opportunity called One Day Internship. It has stores in almost all the big cities in Japan. Students can visit their stores in different cities in Japan and listen to managers' presentation by following the time schedule that the stores offer during the same day. However, it is similar to the so-called internship provided by many travel agencies in Japan. Participants pay a lot of money to the agencies to join a tourism like internship. Needless to say, it is not the real internship but a specialized tour with a sightseeing at the jobsite.

 Internship in Japan does not offer any opportunity to the students to apply their knowledge learned in the classroom to the real world environment. Students do not have a chance to receive the real job discipline or gain experience needed for their future career. University education has duty to train a graduate to have both knowledge and practical experience.

The fact that universities in Japan do not provide meaningful internship are largely due to the traditions of Japanese companies and organizations. Big Japanese companies have their own special training curriculums. As many scholars including Matsushita (2010) and Tanaka (2013) pointed out, Japanese big companies do not expect occupational competence from the college students, even after Health, Labor and Welfare Ministry in Japan officially required university to develop basic occupational competence of Japanese college student. As Matsushita (2010) pointed out, what big companies in Japan expected is the potential to make an effort in future, as which they regard students' test score, but not as their real competence. That is the reason why Tanaka (2013) criticized, Japanese have preferred general education to occupational education. This is evident as the expression made by some Japanese critics against internship from UNIQLO. UNIQLO is a rare company in Japan that adopts the same internship system as the U.S. and other countries. Japanese teachers and companies accused UNIQLO for not allowing the students to concentrate on their study.

However, what is the purpose of study? It is for a student's own life benefit. As Tanaka (2013) explained in details, American universities have a view that education must consider student's future life including a job. Japanese education tends to separate the future job from the necessary training in the universities except the occupational schools. Japanese focus too much on the general education backed by Japanese big companies.

Japanese should have an eye open on the ultimate goal on education. More Japanese work for small and medium-sized business than big ones nowadays. As Suzuki (2014) concluded, Japanese small and medium-sized business companies began to look for work-ready graduate with practical English skills because they do not have money and time to train their new hires now. In other words, most of Japanese business wants work-ready graduate with strong English and occupational skills in the era of globalization. In addition, more and more Japanese students plan to gain overseas work experience. Students in other countries can acquire their skills via internship. Japanese education system should not ignore the fact anymore.

5. English Education and Business English in Japan

Not only internship in Japan but also Business English classes in Japan are not practical and different from the ones from the other countries.

Whether it is Business English, Business Japanese, or Business Chinese, in addition to the basic language skills, the main contents should be the knowledge of business. Business study academically is the business management or business administration study that includes marketing management, finance management, organizational study, and business strategies study. In the U.S., business education teaches the management knowledge to the student at their earlier age. Business classes are offered as early as the junior high. University education curriculum BBA (Bachelor of Business Administration) program is for the undergraduate business students and MBA (Master of Business Administration) program is for the graduate business students. All the business education curriculums share the same contents of learning the fundamental management knowledge. Management concepts are divided by different levels based on students' grade.

It is impossible to provide an accurate definition to the ambiguous Business English class at Japanese university. Author and her school could not discover any educational material that closely ties to the real business management.

Mostly of the material is just English class with some business vocabularies.

There are several kind of business classes in Japanese universities. One of them is the conversational. Students learn only how to make simple responses, exchange business cards, and greetings. It is not a real Business English class but an English greeting class because the business is far beyond the simple greetings. As to the reading and writing, the reading material includes some business elements and students are only required to write an essay using a few business related words.

Learning Business English is not equivalent to learning vocabulary in business scenes. In Business English class, students should learn fundamental business management in English systematically. Learning business means learning the science of business management. Student should learn four basic types of business management, marketing management, finance management, organizational culture, and business strategies in English.[2]

6. Oversea Internship Project and the Effect

To prepare our student to independently and actively live in a globalized society, author and her school have set up oversea internship programs and offer real Business English class by adopting the models from the U.S. and other countries.

In Business English class, author has been teaching student four basic business management systematically in English since three years ago. Students have made field trips to the real international companies, performed cases studies, and come up good solutions by themselves utilizing their marketing management knowledge. Students have successfully learned and used balance sheets and accounting cash flow forms in English. Those experiences can practically help our students to pursue their careers in the globalized world after graduation.

As to overseas internship programs, author and her school have set up real internship opportunities both abroad and with international organizations in Japan. Both of them are real internship programs by American standard. In order to provide a stage to our students, author and her school have determined to build up a project where students can improve their English and gain experience in the real business world. With these goals in mind, author has set up an internship program with Costco Japan and Cordings in England. Both of the programs provide great experiences to our business English classes and fit in our educational curriculums.

Cordings was established in 1839 in London and has a strong history and heritage in British culture and fashion. It is an ideal place for our students to learn not only business but also true British culture and fashion besides authentic English. In its history Cordings has made hunting and shooting goods for the British royal family many times. Our school has sent six students to Cordings for practical training since this program was set up a few years ago. This is a true internship program in western style. Participated students work as a staff in Cordings. Our students have a chance to work for every department at store and office with the opportunities to communicate and provide service to the customers directly. Our students have attended in marketing strategy meetings and presented their creative ideas. They were often asked to provide suggestions to improve Cordings' business.

Work experience at Cordings has strongly increased our students' motivation to study hard in our Business English class. One of our students quit her part time job and focused on studying English over seven hours every day in order to pass the Cordings project interview to have an internship opportunity in London. During one month stay in London, facing new challenges from their work every day, our students deeply involved in their job. They have found efficient ways to finish their jobs and achieve their goals. Gradually, they have not only gained work experience but also greatly improved their language skills. One of the students' TOEIC score has improved from 420 to 800 after she completed her one month internship. Another student has successfully presented her new marketing proposals in English in London. Her proposal was adopted at Cordings marketing meeting.

  The reason that this internship project worked well lies in our focus on the motivation and learner's autonomy in learning English. Lamb (2004), Pavlenco (2002), and Coetzee-Van Rooy (2006) suggested that students aspire to "a vision of an English-speaking globally-involved but nationally responsible future self" (Lamb 2004: 16). Paying attention to the motivation and learner's autonomy in integrating business and English through a meaningful internship is supported by Rogers' (1951, 1969, 1982, 1994) theory that a person is only interested in learnings significantly influenced behavior. Rogers believes it is the most significant learning method. According to Rogers, significant learning takes place when the subject matter is perceived by the student as having relevance to his or her own purposes. In addition, significant learning is acquired through hands on experience. Moreover, learning is facilitated when the student participates responsibly in the learning process. True internship demands students' job responsibility and job learning as well. Learning English also becomes students' responsibility because they have to use English not for chatting with their friends but also communicating with the customers. Responsibility drives student to learn more and learning significantly influence students' behavior. The participants of our internship programs have told us that the reality, seriousness, job responsibilities, English communication, and all the learnings are totally different from the ordinary overseas study.[3]

7. Conclusion

In the U. S. and Singapore, when examining job advertisement in the newspapers and asking the employers in the real world about an ideal candidate, the answers mostly are a candidate with systematic knowledge required by the job and practical experiences. They need a graduate who has completed all the education required by the school and practical experience. It is also becoming a tendency of the Japanese society as it is impacted by the globalization.

Educational institutes have the responsibility to help their graduates to acquire practical knowledge and skills, critical and logic thinking abilities, and effective communication skills. Graduates must go through those accumulative processes at school. Knowing how to exchange business card, greet in English, read business short stories, and write a report with small paragraphs and some business terms do not meet the real business career needs. Business English curriculum in Japanese universities must be improved to allow the students to systematically learn the basic knowledge of marketing management, finance management, and organization studies in English. The best way for the students to acquire business critical thinking is to perform the case studies from the real business world.[4] Students individually or in group study real business cases by utilizing their knowledge learned from the business classes, analyze the internal relationships, and create their own solutions for the real problems. Finally, students should make a presentation about their achievement in English. It helps students to be confident in their abilities and a beneficial for their future career. Students can and should study business not only in the class room but also in work field. Field work can help students to understand what the real business is and what a real business person does.

  The real internship is an intentionally supervised learning related to one's field of study and career goal.

Internship can be a very structured learning experience and can be designed to meet the expectations of the students. It can be done domestically or overseas with the required language trainings. The most important aspects of a true internship are real obligations, job assignments, and duties to participators. Receiving education only on campus is not enough to allow the graduates to perform at high level in the real world environment. Good graduates must have both interpersonal skills and leadership qualities. In addition to obtain valuable work experiences from the internship programs, students can also build up their confidence, critical thinking ability, and make quick decisions based on the reasoning. Students' oral communication skills and language ability can be improved too. In addition, students' motivation to study is increased. Moreover, students can build good work habits, establish network, and build great resume for their future career. These advantages, of course, rely on a true internship and true Business English.

This paper is based on the manuscript of the author's presentation entitled "True or False? Business English and

Internship in Japan," in the symposium of "A Crossover Point between Abilities of Working and English Communication," at Nagoya Institute of Technology, Nagoya, Japan, December 19, 2014.

Notes

[1] Several proposals were made to the educational world, for instance, "Employability" by Japan Business Federation (Keidanren) in 1999, "Basic Abilities for Employment" by Ministry of Health, Labor and Welfare in 2004, and "Basic Abilities as A Member of Society" by Ministry of Economy, Trade and Industry in 2006.

[2] As to the concrete pedagogy in classes in Japan and the effect for Japanese student, see Kuwamura (2013).

[3] See Kuwamura (2013).

[4] See Kuwamura (2013).

Bibliography

Coetzee-Van Rooy, S. (2006) Integrativeness: Untenable for world Englishes learners? *World Englishes* 25, 3/4, 437-450.

Kuwamra, T. (2013) English education with use of adaptation strategy: To train the ability to think and to use English with eye on cultural diversity. ("Tekiōsenryaku" wo mochiita eigokyōiku — Bungateki tayōsei eno manazashi wo motta shikōryoku to eigoryoku no tameni.) *Leornian* 17, 33-42.

Lamb, M. (2004) Integrative motivation in a globalizing world. *System* 32, 3-19.

Matsushita, K. (2010) The concept of "new abilities" and education. (<Atarashii nōryoku> gainen to kyōiku.) Matsuhita, K. (ed.) *Can "New Abilities" Change Education?: Academic Ability, Literacy, Competency.* (*<Atarashii nōryoku> wa kyōiku wo kaeruka—Gakuryoku・literashī・konpetenshī.*) Minerva Shobō, 1-42.

Pavlenko, A. (2002) Poststructuralist approaches to the study of social factors in second language learning and use. V. Cook (ed.) *Portraits of the L2 User.* Clevedon: Multilingual Matters, 277-302.

Rogers, C. (1951) *Client-centered Therapy: Its Current Practice, Implications and Theory.* London: Constable.

Rogers, C. (1969) *Freedom to Learn: A View of What Education Might Become.* Columbus: Charles Merrill.

Rogers, C. (1982) Freedom to Learn for the 80's. Columbus: Charles Merrill.

Rogers, C. and Freiberg, H. J. (1994) *Freedom to Learn* (3rd Edition). New York: Pearson.

Suzuki, A. (2014) Need for Anglophone literature for Japanese students in a globalized society: Developing a resilient life. *Lit Matters*, Summer 2014 1(1), 86-106.

Tanaka, K. (2013) *Why Does Not "Occupational Education" Take Root?: Occupation and Work Alienation in the Constitution and the Education Act.* (*"Shokugyō kyōiku wa naze nezukanainoka ― Kenpō・kyōikuhō no nakano shokugyō・Rōdōsogai.*) Akashi Shoten.

Why E-learning materials fail

Kelly Quinn

The effectiveness of online materials has been the subject of some controversy. Swan (2003) says, "students generally learn as much online as they do in traditional classroom environments." In contrast, Welsh et al (2003) suggest that claims about the efficiency and success of e-learning materials should be "regarded with caution." One problem that arises with evaluating the effectiveness of e-learning materials is that traditional materials and e-learning materials are rarely compared side-by-side. This paper describes two situations that allowed for the direct comparison of the two methods of presenting materials, but resulted in opposite outcomes. At a national Japanese public university in 2011, when comparing the results of an end of semester common test, it was seen that students using the online versions of textbook activities regularly outperformed students completing the same activities using only the textbook. In 2013 the opposite result occurred at a private university. In this case, students that combined traditional workbooks with in class assessment outperformed students using the online materials. These conflicting results can be explained by recognizing the importance of immediacy and the interaction between the student, teachers, and peers, as described in Shea et al (2002). Students who perceive themselves to have strong, positive interactions with classmates and teachers reported the best learning outcomes. Teachers hoping to effectively incorporate online materials into their courses need to be aware of the importance of the interactions between and among teachers and students and ensure that those interactions are preserved online.

Background to Success

The drill activities from the textbook at the public university were converted to Moodle activities and made available on the school's server. Thus, there were two groups of students. The first group used only the textbook. The second group had the same textbook, but they could also access the same textbook activities as e-learning activities using MOODLE, an open source e-learning system. Students were able to access the activities either at school or from their homes or using their smart phones.

Before classes began, students took the Test of English for International Communication (TOEIC) and were sorted into classes based on their TOEIC score. Approximately one thousand students were divided into classes of about forty students. In 2011 the top score on TOEIC by an incoming student was 900 points, combined listening and writing. The lowest was 180 points. According to the TOEIC Users Guide, students with scores in the 860 – 990 range, have the "ability to communicate on a variety of topics and are reasonably accurate and understandable." On the other hand, students with scores below 220 are described as, "ability to communicate in English very limited."

Even though the textbook and materials were the same regardless of level, it was expected that students of similar level would complete activities around the same time and that the flow and time management of the class would be easier. Also, because the students were streamed into different classes based on ability, it was possible to compare final exam scores of students with the same ability and compare their performance on the final exam.

The final factor that allowed the comparison to take place was the use of a common final exam. After completing five units of the textbook, all teachers teaching the course administered the same exam. Because the test was based directly on the textbook, it would reveal how well students had mastered that material and would allow teachers to see which method of delivery, MOODLE or textbook, helped students more.

Data

The data in this study was collected from students in the class English for Science and Technology I. Students were divided into classes based on their TOEIC scores. All students used the same textbook and all students took the same end of semester final exam. Data of the project is summarized in Table 1.

Table 1. Summary of Key Data

English for Science & Technology Period 3			
Level	MOODLE	TOEIC	Final Exam Score
Level-1	YES	655	81.27
Level-2	NO	546	77.54
Level-3	NO	513	76.2
Level-4	YES	490	78.16
Level-5	YES	473	74.60
Level-6	NO	456	67.58
Level-7	NO	438	72.40
Level-8	NO	423	68.30
Level-9	NO	408	70.58
Level-10	YES	385	73.03
Level-11	NO	360	68.89
Level-12	YES	326	69.52
Level-13	YES	254	57.47

English for Science & Technology Period 4			
Level	MOODLE	TOEIC	Final Exam Score
Level-1	NO	669	79.19
Level-2	NO	542	77.28
Level-3	YES	504	76.30
Level-4	NO	484	72.65
Level-5	YES	463	72.71
Level-6	YES	444	73.05
Level-7	NO	430	72.4
Level-8	NO	410	70.58
Level-9	NO	394	69.14
Level-10	YES	378	74.24
Level-11	NO	356	67.17
Level-12	YES	327	70.09
Level-13	YES	282	65.78

Results and Discussion

MOODLE activities were used in twelve of the twenty-six classes. The most interesting comparison is between adjacent classes where one class used the MOODLE materials and the class either immediately above or below did not. This situation occurred ten times. There were seven instances where the higher level class did not use the MOODLE activities while the class immediately below them in level did. Of these seven instances, students in the lower MOODLE class outperformed students in the higher level non-MOODLE class six of the seven times. For example, in Period 3, students in the Level-3 class had an average TOEIC score of 513 and an average final exam score of 76.2. Students in the Level-4 class had an average TOEIC score of 490 and an average final exam score of 78.16. In fact, students in the Level-4 class outperformed not only the class immediately above them, Level-3, but also achieved a higher average score than the students in the Level-2 class who had a significantly higher TOEIC score, 546 in Level-2 versus 490 in Level-4.

In no instances did students in non-MOODLE class outperform students of higher ability who had used MOODLE. In fact, in only one instance did students in a non-MOODLE class outperform students in the level below them when the students were using the MOODLE activities. In Period 4, the students in Level-2 did not use MOODLE while the students in Level-3 below them did. In this case the higher level students outscored the MOODLE using students. However, it is interesting to note that even though the students in Level-3 did not outperform the students immediately above them, they did achieve a higher average score than the Level-3 class in Period 3 who had roughly the same TOEIC score. Students in Period 3, Level-3 had a TOEIC score of 513 and achieved an average score of 76.2 on the final exam. Students in Period 4, Level-3 had a TOEIC score of 504 points, slightly lower than Period 3, and achieved an average score of 76.30 on the final exam.

Background to Failure

The second study dealt with students' mastery of items from the Academic Word List (AWL). At the beginning of the semester, in both the paper-based and Moodle classes, students were given a pretest. The pretest included the material and type of activities used in the activities: definition matching, word form chart completion, and fill-in-the-blank exercises. At the end of the semester, the same test was given as a posttest to determine to what degree students had mastered the skills and materials presented in the activities during the semester.

In the first semester, the paper-based activities included two types of activities: definition matching and fill-in-the-blank activities. Students were given 20 words every two weeks and made vocabulary cards for them which were to include the English and Japanese definitions, each word's part of speech, other parts of speech of the word, and a sample sentence. Students reviewed the words in pairs at the start of each class for five minutes. Students were given a definition matching exercise as homework to help practice learning the words in context. A week later, students were quizzed to match definitions of each word from a list of four options and to complete a word form chart. The following week, students were given a fill in the blank activity in which students had to select the correct word and its correct part of speech to complete each sentence similar to the one they had done as practice. Students were given a midterm of the first 60 words and a comprehensive exam at the end of the semester. Students also sometimes played vocabulary games where they had to identify different parts of speech of targeted vocabulary by writing words on the board. This was also done to reinforce correct spelling.

    In the first semester, the Moodle activities included three types of activities: a definition matching activity, a word form activity, and a fill in the blank activity. The AWL does not include definitions or word form information so the first thing to do was to teach the students the most common English definitions for the words. Students were given an English definition and then had to choose the most appropriate word to match the definition. If a word had multiple definitions or if the meaning of the word significantly changed for different word forms, an additional quiz problem was included for each meaning. For the word form activity, students had to change the form of the head word to its different forms. For example, students were given the word "accumulate" and asked to write the noun form "accumulation" and the past participle form "accumulated." Word forms that indicated people and forms that used prefixes to make forms with opposite meanings were also required. For example, students were prompted to provide the opposite form of the word "accurate," "inaccurate." For the fill in the blank activity, students were provided with scrambled versions of the head words. They had to unscramble the words and change the use the correct form of the word to complete a sentence. Two quizzes were given during the semester in both the paper-based class and the Moodle class and at the end of the semester a comprehensive exam was given.

In the second semester, both the paper-based activities and the Moodle activities were revised. In the second semester, the types of activities and the content of the activities were identical. In addition to the definition, word form and fill in the blank activities of the first semester, error correction and collocation activities were added. The activities were collected into a workbook and provided to the students. In the paper-based class, students would complete the workbook activities on their own as homework and then in class check the answers in small groups or ask the teacher for the answers to problems that they were unsure of.

In the Moodle class, students downloaded a pdf of the

workbook activities which they could use offline, but to check their answers, they had to access the online version on the Moodle site. No answers were given in class and except when the students encountered some technical issue with the Moodle site, no class time was committed to the vocabulary activities.

Results of first semester pretest and posttest

The results of the pretest and posttest scores for the first semester are summarized in Table 1 and Table 2 below. In both the paper-based and Moodle activities students showed improvement, +57% (paper-based) and +52% (Moodle) respectively. While the difference between the two groups is not large, it is interesting to note that students in the paper-based class (class average of 75%) outperformed students in the Moodle class (class average of 69%).

Table 1. Teacher 1: In class, paper-based material results

Student No.	Pretest Score (%)	Posttest Score (%)	Change (%)
Student 1	4	62	58
Student 2	26	68	42
Student 3	28	76	48
Student 4	22	68	46

Student 5	8	76	68
Student 6	20	86	66
Student 7	12	70	58
Student 8	12	78	66
Student 9	*	64	*
Student 10	12	86	74
Student 11	36	80	44
Student 12	12	80	68
Student 13	18	84	66
Student 14	10	58	48
Student 15	*	*	*
Student 16	36	92	56
Student 17	18	72	54
	Average	Average	Average
	18	75	57%

* Student did not take the test.

Table 2. Teacher 2: Outside class, Moodle-based material results

Student No.	Pretest Score (%)	Posttest Score (%)	Change (%)
Student 1	12	82	70
Student 2	*	58	*

Student 3	20	66	46
Student 4	16	74	68
Student 5	20	70	50
Student 6	12	74	62
Student 7	28	42	14
Student 8	16	84	68
Student 9	16	56	40
Student 10	28	68	40
Student 11	4	82	78
Student 12	12	80	68
Student 13	4	54	50
Student 14	20	40	20
Student 15	24	94	70
Student 16	4	56	52
Student 17	8	76	68
Student 18	48	82	34
	Average (%)	Average (%)	Average (%)
	17	69	52

Results of second semester pretest and posttest

The results of the pretest and posttest scores for the second semester are summarized in Table 3 and Table 4 below.

The results of the first semester were confirmed in the second. Students in the paper-based class (class average of 78%) slightly outperformed students in the Moodle class (class average of 72%). In the second semester students in both classes had higher pretest scores than in the first semester and the average score was the same in both classes, 34%. The higher pretest scores could be due to greater familiarity with the style of questions in the test or perhaps to an increase in vocabulary knowledge developed through other course work and activities. In any case, because of the higher pretest scores, the percent of change was less in the second semester than in the first even though the scores on the posttest were on average higher.

Table 3. Teacher 1: Workbook with in-class answer checking

Student No.	Pretest Score (%)	Posttest Score (%)	Change (%)
Student 1	22	66	44
Student 2	48	85	37
Student 3	51	81	30
Student 4	22	74	52
Student 5	37	81	44

Student 6	22	92	70
Student 7	29	85	56
Student 8	37	77	40
Student 9	25	92	67
Student 10	44	66	22
Student 11	44	62	18
Student 12	29	85	56
Student 13	40	77	37
Student 14	29	48	19
Student 15	33	81	48
Student 16	29	96	67
	Average (%)	Average (%)	Average (%)
	34	78	44

Table 4. Teacher 2: Outside class workbook with online self-checking

Student No.	Pretest Score (%)	Posttest Score (%)	Change (%)
Student 1	30	93	63
Student 2	33	56	23
Student 3	48	67	19
Student 4	44	70	26

Student 5	22	74	52
Student 6	48	82	34
Student 7	30	74	44
Student 8	63	93	30
Student 9	15	74	59
Student 10	19	56	37
Student 11	37	85	48
Student 12	33	85	52
Student 13	22	52	30
Student 14	33	56	23
Student 15	26	56	30
	Average (%)	Average (%)	Average (%)
	34	72	38

Conclusion

In conclusion, students in classes where the material was used in class performed slightly better than students who dealt with the material strictly out of class. In fact, the difference of in class activities and out of class activities may be more important than the difference between the methods of delivery of the materials whether online or paper-based. By doing the activities in class, teachers demonstrate their importance and peer pressure from classmates can motivate students to keep up with the activities in a way that online activities which students are left to do by themselves might not. Still, because the overall scores were so similar, advocates of the benefits of online learning can be encouraged that results roughly equal to those obtained through classroom work can be obtained online.

References

Coxhead, A. (2000). A new academic word list. *TESOL Quarterly, 34*(2): 213-238.

Laufer, B. (1989). What percentage of text-lexis is essential for comprehension? In C. Lauren & M. Nordman (Eds.) *Special Language: From Humans Thinking to Thinking Machines* (pp.69-75). Clevedon: Multilingual Matters.

Laufer, B. (2003). Vocabulary acquisition in a second language: Do learners really acquire most vocabulary by reading? Some empirical evidence. Canadian Modern Language Review, 59(4): 565-585.

Melka, T. F. (1997). Receptive versus productive aspects of vocabulary. In N. Schmitt & M. McCarthy (Eds.) *Vocabulary: Description, Acquisition and Pedagogy* (pp. 6-19). Cambridge: Cambridge.

Na, L. and Nation, P. (1985). Factors affecting guessing vocabulary in context. *RELC Journal 16*: 33-42.

Nagy, W. E. (1985). Learning words from context. *Reading Research Quarterly 20*: 233-253.

Nation, P. (1990). *Teaching and Learning Vocabulary.* New York: Newbury House.

Nation, P. & Waring, R. (1997). Vocabulary size, text coverage and word lists. In N. Schmitt & M. McCarthy (Eds.) *Vocabulary: Description, Acquisition and Pedagogy* (pp. 6-19). Cambridge: Cambridge.

Schatz, E. K. & Baldwin, R. S. (1986). Context clues are unreliable predictors of word meanings. *Reading Research Quarterly, 21*: 439-453.

Shea, P. J., Swan, K., Fredericksen, E. E & Pickett, A. M. (2002). Student satisfaction and reported learning in the SUNY Learning Network. In J. Bourne & J. C. Moore (Eds) Elements of Quality Online Education, Volume 3. Olin and Babson Colleges: Sloan Center for Online Education.

Sternberg, R. (1987). Most vocabulary is learned through context. In M. G. McKeown and M. E. Curtis (Eds.) *The Nature of Vocabulary Acquisition* (pp. 89-105). Hillsdale, NJ: Erlbaum.

Swan, K. (2003). Learning effectiveness: what the research tells us. In J. Bourne & J. C. Moore (Eds) Elements of Quality Online Education, Practice and Direction. Needham, MA: Sloan Center for Online Education, 13-45.

Welsh, E. T., Wanberg, C. R., Brown, K. G. and Simmering, M. J. (2003), E-learning: emerging uses, empirical results and future directions. International Journal of Training and Development, 7, 245–258.

West, M. (1953). A general service list of English words. London: Longman, Green and Company.

Zimmerman, C. B. (1997). Historical trends in second language vocabulary instruction. *Second language vocabulary acquisition*, 5-19.

Mastering English Skills for Professional Success: Reading Materials

Masashi Nagai
nagai@nitech.ac.jp
Nagoya Institute of Technology

Keywords: English skill, reading material, career development, professional success

Mastering English skills for professional success requires materials well-grounded on theoretical and practical considerations. The present paper discusses reading materials conducive to the goal, and suggests some sample topics which are arguably instrumental to it. Beginning with the discussion of professional skills which are highly valued by those people who work in business, we seek to optimize collegiate English reading materials for career development.*

1. Professional Skills in Business Environments

Many businesspersons, including Iga (2012) and Tozuka

(2013) who have worked for McKinsey & Company, Inc., a consulting firm with branches across the world, discuss basic skills necessary for the globalized business environments, and point out (in essence) the following.

1. Leadership
2. Logical Thinking (Critical Thinking)
3. English command

Leadership is not to be taken as just getting ahead of others. It is the state of mind ready to state one's position when necessary and bring about changes in the real world. It is ranked well above logical thinking and English command.
Logical thinking involves technicalities instantiated by MECE (mutually exclusive and collectively exhaustive) and others, and also shares much with critical thinking. Critical thinking, by its very definition, examines every phenomenon critically without any bias (preconception).
The command of English deemed essential by the authors above and others is the ability to articulate one's opinion in English and communicate effectively. It does not necessarily require fluency, native accent, etc.
Bearing in mind the above mentioned state of affairs, we owe

it to ourselves to introduce logical (or critical) thinking training into English education for non-native speakers.

2. Reading Materials Suggested

We provide below some suggestive reading materials for fostering critical thinking attitudes in English education environments (for the ease of discussion we confine ourselves to the field of scientific English below).

Government and Scientific Community

Two scientific journals have come under pressure from the US government not to publish findings of research on the highly infectious strains (H5N1) of the bird flu virus over fears that terrorists could use the information to create bioweapons. Critics argue that keeping the science secret could hamper efforts to find new vaccines and drugs to combat an infectious form of human H5N1.

Some researchers warn that although they would respect the government's request, it may be too late to stop the spread of the research findings as scientific data has already been shared with hundreds of researchers and governments in open meetings.

(Source: telegraph.co.uk, 2011/12/22)

Controversy regarding Bioethics

Recent advances in genetics has enabled the creation of a designer baby, a baby whose genetic makeup is artificially selected by genetic engineering combined with in vitro fertilization to ensure the presence or absence of particular genes or characteristics.

Opponents of the designer baby argue that genetic enhancements may change our descendants to such an extent that they lose their humanity. They claim that environmental influences operate only within limits set by genes, meaning that even ambitious education programs leave their subjects' humanity intact. Moral and ethical questions about a license to design babies concern the kind of societies it might lead to. Liberal democracy is a cooperative activity in which everyone is seen as having something to offer. Genetic enhancement may bring this social arrangement to an end, creating societies in which unenhanced people are viewed by their genetic superiors as useless.

(Source: actionbioscience.org)

Controversy regarding Public Interest

Verdant, California has seen an increased traffic flow on

many secondary roads in the area due to population growth. Some of the trees along the roads are quite close to the pavement, and law suits have been filed against the road commission for not maintaining sufficient road safety. Officials concerned about safety as well as law suits have planned to widen the roads, but this requires cutting down many healthy, longstanding trees along the roads.

A citizen environmental group complains, "Accidents are the fault of careless drivers. Cutting down trees to protect drivers from their own carelessness symbolizes the destruction of our natural environment for the sake of human 'progress.' It's time to turn things around. Sue the drivers if they don't drive sensibly." Many letters on both sides of the issue appear in the local newspaper.
(Source: The Online Ethics Center, Center for Engineering Ethics and Society)

Scientific Misconduct

The investigating committee at the University of Tokyo announced that one of the experiments performed by a Japanese RNA researcher, whose credibility stands in doubt, has failed a first test to reproduce the results. This was in response to a number of complaints from international researchers that they could not reproduce the experimental results. The investigating committee first asked the researcher to submit raw data, but he could not do so. His assistant admitted that he had not kept his notebooks. It also seems that some data stored in a computer had been deleted

Although officials from the university did not discuss whether scientific fraud or fabrication was involved, the spokesperson for the committee said "there are many things that look doubtful."

(Source: nature.com, 2006/1/27)

Engineering Ethics— organizational culture

The Space Shuttle *Columbia* disaster occurred in 2003 during re-entry into the Earth's atmosphere, resulting in the death of all seven crew members. The loss of *Columbia* was a result of damage sustained during launch when a piece of foam insulation broke off from the external tank.

The accident investigation board delved deeply into the underlying organizational and cultural issues that led to the accident. Their report criticized NASA's decision-making and risk-assessment processes. It concluded the organizational structure and processes were sufficiently flawed and that compromise of safety was expected no matter who was in the key decision-making positions. An example was the position of Shuttle Program Manager, where one individual was responsible for achieving safe, timely launches and acceptable costs, which are often conflicting goals. The board made recommendations for significant changes in processes and organizational culture.

(Source: Wikipedia)

Engineering Ethics— trading off safety for cost.

The Ford Pinto, subcompact automobile produced by the Ford Motor Company, is famous for the controversy surrounding the safety of its fuel tank design and Ford's recall of the car.

[3]Critics alleged that the vehicle's lack of reinforcing structure between the rear panel and the tank meant the tank would be pushed forward and punctured by the protruding bolts of the differential — making the car less safe than other cars of its class.

Ford allegedly was aware of the design flaw, refused to pay for a redesign, and decided it would be cheaper to pay off possible lawsuits for resulting deaths. Ford used a cost-benefit analysis to compare the cost of an $11 repair against the monetary value of a human life. Apparently, Ford traded off safety for cost.

(Source: Wikipedia)

Engineering Ethics—false sense of safety

BP oil spill, the worst man-made environmental disaster in U.S. history, occurred when gas surged upward from the well below the Gulf of Mexico and exploded, killing 11 workers, injuring 17, and polluting the ocean with more than 170 million gallons of oil.

From "fail-safe" measures that failed to unheeded warnings, inadequate inspections, and unstable cement, the Gulf oil spill provides a series of teachable moments -technical, theoretical, and professional.

The most important lesson from the calamity is that people can at times be the weakest links in the system. There was increasing sense of false safety, that they have been doing something so long and gotten away with it so many times that what they do is therefore inherently safe.

(Source: ASEE Prism, American Society for Engineering
Education)

3. Concluding Remarks

The present paper dealt with English in terms of

professional skills and provided the rationale and some specifics of reading materials which are conducive to fostering critical thinking environments in the ESP instruction. It is hoped that this paper will serve as a good starting point for the ESP students, teachers, and researchers.

*Part of the materials contained in this paper overlaps with what I have argued elsewhere.

Bibliography

Iga, Yasuyo (2012) *Saiyo-Kijun* (Recruitment Standards), Diamond Press, Tokyo.

McInerny, D. Q. (2005) *Being Logical,* Random House, New York.

Nagai, Masashi (2015, in press) "Concepts and Materials in ESP," *Katahira* 50.

Nagai, Masashi (2013) "Critical Thinking Approach to Teaching English for Engineering," Proceedings of the First International Conference on Teaching English for Specific Purposes, Niš, Serbia.

Nagai, Masashi, Kelly Quinn, Brian Cullen (2012) *Critical Thinking Skills for Engineering Students,* Komura, Nagoya Institute of Technology.

Tozuka, Takamasa (2013) *Sekai-no Erito-ha Naze Kono Kihon-wo Daijinisurunoka* (The workplace basics for global business), Asahi Shimbun Press, Tokyo.

Weston, Anthony (2008) *A Rulebook for Arguments,* Hackett Publishing, Indianapolis.

APPENDIX

「仕事に役立つ英語」とは

1　グローバル人材をめぐる議論

2　大学と職業訓練（実用英語/科学技術英語）

3　実際の取り組み

マッキンゼー流の人材論

1　リーダーシップ

2　論理的思考力（批判的思考力）

3　英語力

伊賀泰代(2012), 戸塚隆将(2013), etc.

大学と実用英語/科学技術英語

- Education as <u>Knowledge-Building</u>
- Education as <u>Habit-Formation</u>

Harry D. Kitson (2004), etc.

工学部における英語教育

英語教科書の現状

(1) science non-fiction—139 books
(2) technical English—22 books

（データ出典：大学英語教科書協会目録）

Critical Thinking Skills for Engineering Students

新しい教科書

Critical Thinking Skills for Engineering Students
(Nagai, Quinn, Cullen, 2012)

学部2年 前期(選択科目)
「総合英語」

単元の例(1)

- Chapter 1: Space Shuttle Disaster—What Went Wrong?
- Chapter 2: Ford Pinto's Case—Safety or Cost?
- Chapter 3: BP Oil Spill—Learning From Disaster

単元の例(2)

- Chapter 4: Designer Baby—A Dream Come True?
- Chapter 5: Controlling Research Into Deadly Virus
- Chapter 6: Experiments Found Impossible To Repeat

章末課題の例 – Space Shuttle Disaster

The text ends with the sentence "The board made recommendations for significant changes in processes and organizational culture."
What do you think can be done to prevent accidents like the one in the text from happening again in the future?

章末課題の例 – Ford Pinto's Case

The text mentions "public dissatisfaction with risk-damage assessments where human lives are involved."
What do you think about manufacturers trading off safety for cost? Is it a necessary evil?

【実践報告】

名古屋工業大学海外交流の試み
―平成 26 年度海外語学研修活動報告―

松浦千佳子

1. はじめに―名古屋工業大学の海外交流プログラム

名古屋工業大学（以下本学）では、平成 26 年度現在、①交換留学、②海外インターンシップ、③情報・電子電気系専門プログラム、そして④海外語学研修の 4 種類の海外交流プログラムを実施している。以下に各プログラムについて簡単に述べる。

1.1 交換留学

交換留学は学生交流提携校とのプログラムで、対象は学部生および大学院生である。留学期間は 1 年を上限で、その間、講義を履修、または研究指導を受けることになる。受け入れ先は 27 か国・地域の 58 校で、うち授業料不徴収校は 17 か国 34 校である。

近年では、フィンランドのアールト大学、オーストラリアのシドニー工科大学、フランスのリール国立化学大学院、スペインのバレンシア州立工芸大学などに学部生・大学院生を送り出している。

人気が高いのは、フィンランドやオーストラリアなど英語で学べるところではあるが、語学研修が目的のプログラムはないため、講義が理解できるだけの語学力が前提となる。また、非英語圏の場合、英語で行われている講義は限られているので講義履修が中心となる学部生にはハードルはかなり高い。また、学業成績も優秀であることが必要条件となる。

ここ数年、本学でも留学への関心が高くなり、年に数名のレベルではあるが、TOEFL や IELTS で留学基準を満たした、意欲ある学生が応募するようになっている。なお、留学希望者の面接は英語担当教員が行い、語学力・動機などの確認を行っている。

1.2　海外インターンシップ
　海外インターンシップは、平成17～21年度の「産学提携による実践型人材育成事業」に基づいて設けられた。
　受け入れ先は、ドイツ Coburg にある自動車部品メーカーの Brose 社と、本学とゆかりのある合衆国のイムラ社である。対象学生は博士前期課程の学生2名（物質工学または機能工学専攻など）で夏季休暇中の2か月を利用して行う。英語力の基準は TOEIC600 点以上で、使用言語は英語、渡航費・滞在は各社の負担である。

1.3　情報・電子電気系専門プログラム
　情報・電子電気系の学部生・大学院生に特化した短期のフランスでのプログラムが2つある。
　まず、情報系の学部生を対象に EFREI で3月に実施するコース、そして情報・電子電気系大学院生を対象に ESIGELEC で9月に行われるコースだ。いずれも、本学学生のために英語で開講する1か月のプログラムで、学術交流協定により学費は免除され、単位も認定している。

1.4　海外語学研修
　前述の2と3は専門教員が主体となった専門性の強いプログラムだが、海外語学研修プログラムは英語担当教員が主体となり、留学生支援室の事務的支援を得て実施している。
　受け入れ先は、連合王国マンチェスター大学と合衆国メリルハースト大学の2校で、夏季休暇中の4週間、現地の英語研修コースに参加する形式で実施している。対象は学部1～3年次で、初めて海外に行く学生、実践的な英語力を身につけたい学生、海外経験には興味がある

が長期留学の余裕がない学生が主となっている。前述の3つのプログラムの準備過程、海外交流の最初のステップという位置づけと考えてよいだろう。

2. 海外語学研修プログラム

本プログラムの発端は、平成17～19年度に採択された現代的教育ニーズ取り組み支援プログラム（現代GP）（仕事で英語が使える日本人の育成）「発信型国際技術者育成のための国学英語教育」プロジェクトだ。

同プロジェクトでは English for General Science & Technology (EGST) 教育を確立させ、ネイティブ講師による少人数 Intensive Course の開講、e-learning 教育の充実、工学専門科目の英語化推進を進めると同時に、海外実践を充実させた。その中で、「実用性の高い英語運用能力を習得することによって、国際社会で活躍できる技術者を育成する」ことを目的に、本学英語教員が主体となって海外語学研修プログラムを構築した。

2.1 経緯

まず、平成17年度に学生アンケートを実施して、開催国・時期・期間など学生の意向を調査した。その結果受けて、連合王国マンチェスター大学・エジンバラ大学、オーストラリアのシドニー大学・メルボルン大学・モナシュ大学・メルボルン工科大学、カナダのブリティッシュコロンビア大学、ニュージーランドのオークランド工科大学・ヴィクトリア大学などで調査を行った。

そこで、本学の学生だけが固まって授業を受けるのではなく、できるだけ色々な国の学生と一緒に学習でき、さらに工学的色彩のある授業も可能な受け入れ先ということで、連合王国マンチェスター大学を選定した。平成18年度の試行を経て、平成19年度よりマンチェスター大学との共同企画により、また本学留学支援室による事務手続きの

支援を得て実施している。

　平成24年度からは合衆国メリルハースト大学でのコースを追加するとともに、対象学生を当初の3年次のみから1〜3年次に拡大した。参加条件はTOEIC500点以上、または英検2級である。

　プログラムは、約10回の事前研修、4週間の現地語学研修、そして帰国後の事後報告会の3段構えとなっており、希望者には3年次英語（選択）科目「英語演習a、b」（1または2単位）を単位認定している。

2.2　実施概要

　4月のオリエンテーションで学生に周知した後に申し込み受け付けを始め、5月のゴールデンウィーク明けに参加者を確定して、ほぼ毎週事前研修会を行う。事前研修会では、参加者間の人間関係作りから、出入国などに関する情報提供、また交通・買い物・食事などの現地情報、トラブル対策、健康管理等について必要知識を深め、どう対応していくかを学ぶ。単なる旅行ガイドにならないよう、参加者各自が、それぞれの場面で、「何のために」、「どうやって」、「何を」話したらいいのか考えられるようにしている。

　マンチェスター大学の受け入れ母体は同語学センターで、授業はEnglish for University Studiesという同大学が通常夏の期間提供しているコースである。これは、英国の大学進学を考えている学生を対象としたコースなので、学習意欲の高い他国の学生と交われる可能性が高い。さらに、このプログラムには、プロジェクト科目（選択）が組み込まれているので、環境・建築など工学系のプロジェクト科目を1つは設定するように依頼している。もちろん、本学以外の学生も選択可能だ。宿泊はマンチェスター大学学寮で、参加学生は原則他国の学生と同じフラットで自炊・生活できるよう配慮されている。

　メリルハースト大学はオレゴン州ポートランド郊外にあるカトリック系の大学で、受け入れ母体は、同大学進学希望者の語学研修を委託されているPacific International Academyだ。授業は、月〜木はAction Projectという、授業に加えてポートランド近郊の様々な場

所・催し物に出かけて生の英語に触れて学ぶコースを受講する。金曜日にはTOEICのクラスで、発音や文法を学ぶ。宿泊はホームステイで、原則、他国の学生と一緒に生活できるよう配慮されている。

　いずれの場合も、当初は、帰国後に面接を行っていたが、平成24年度より全学に周知をして帰国後報告会を開催している。使用言語は特に設定しないで始めたのだが、学生の意欲を買って、平成25年度からは英語による報告会としている。参加目的・成果は様々だが、どの学生も、自分なりに英語を使ってみることで自信をつけ、成長したことがうかがえる。

　なお、参加状況は、平成24年度がマンチェスター大学7名(3年次)、メリルハースト大学6名（3年次）、平成25年度がマンチェスター大学12名（2年次7名、3年次5名）、メリルハースト大学7名（1年次3名、2年次4名）、平成26年度がマンチェスター大学8名（2年次5名、3年次3名）、メリルハースト大学3名（2年次2名、3年次1名）となっている。

2.3　学生からのフィードバック

　参加学生には、帰国後にアンケート調査を行ってプログラムの改善に役立てるとともに、次年度参加者への参考資料としている。

　平成26年度の成果として挙げられているのは、「英語を使うことに慣れた」、「話せる英語にバリエーションが出た」、「発音がうまくなった」、「勉強の習慣がついた」という英語使用に関するもの、そして、「下手な英語でも伝わることが分かり、自信がついた」というコミュニケーションに関わるもの、また、「いろいろな価値観や考え方を知ることで、視野やモノの見方が広がった上に、自分の行動の積極性が増した」という考え方に関わるものだった。英語の授業だけでなく、実際に生活・社会の中で英語を使う体験から学ぶことは、今後の大きな糧になると考えられる。

学生が挙げた反省点としては、「英語力が格段に上がったとは思っていないが、これからどう学んでいくべきなのかという見通しはより明確になった」、「もっとリスニング力などをつけていけばよかった」、「事前に英語の勉強など全くしなかったこと」などという準備学習に関するものと、「日本人でかたまってしゃべってしまう時があったこと」、「日本語を使いすぎてしまった」、「もう少し外に出て外国人と話す機会を増やすべきだった」、「もっと積極的に行動できたらよかった」という現地での言語使用・行動に関するものだった。日本での学習経験が極めて受動的であるということを痛感するとともに、学生がもう少し積極的に話したり、動いたりしなければならない環境を設定していくことが必要だと考えられた。

3．今後の試み

　前述の参加学生からのフィードバックを踏まえ、また、平成26年夏のメリルハースト大学訪問による打ち合わせから、手始めに平成27年度の合衆国プログラムで、サービス・ラーニング・プログラムを取り入れることを検討している。

　サービス・ラーニングという用語は、日本でいうところのインターンシップにあたる。合衆国でインターンシップというのは見習社員であり、短期間で英語もそれほど堪能でない学生の受け入れは事実上不可能だ。そこで、最近では、語学研修と組み合わせて、NGO団体等の職場体験をさせて、実践的な英語力の向上、地域との関わり、より深い社会・文化体験、職場体験をさせるプログラム、サービス・ラーニング・プログラムを組むところが多くなっている。

　メリルハースト大学も例外ではなく、オレゴン州ポートランドのNGO団体での職場体験プログラムを組んでおり、夏季休暇中の4週間でも受講可能となっている。

　具体的には、月曜日から木曜日まで英語の集中講義を受けると同時に職場でのコミュニケーションやアメリカ文化を学び、金曜日にはボ

ランティア体験をするというものである。ボランティア体験は①事前調査、②現地NGO職員の補助作業（グループ単位）、③ボランティア体験についてディスカッションという3つの要素からなり、言語表現に加えて、社会問題についても学習するというものである。

　たとえばホームレスに給食配膳を行うNGOであれば、事前にホームレスについて調査を行う。そして、現実にNGOでホームレスの給食配膳を手伝い、その後、ディスカッションをする。通常、走っているプログラムなので、グループが本学の学生だけで構成されることはない。

　わずか4週間のプログラムであるので、実際に行えることは限られるが、少なくとも現地でより色々な人に触れて、関わることが可能となり、より実践的な英語、コミュニケーション能力が身に付けられるのではないかと考える。

4. 終わりに

　4週間の語学研修で英語力が格段に向上するということは、学生自身もはじめから期待しているわけではないが、実際に語学研修に参加して学習意欲がわき、TOEICで高得点を獲得している学生は少なくない。基本的なことは中高までで学んでわけなのだから、適切な環境と刺激にある期間触れることで運用が飛躍的に伸びるのではないかと考えられる。また、どのプログラムでも、本学の学生は大変まじめで優秀であるとの評価も定着している。

　海外に送り出すだけでなく、日本でも、授業外で英語を使う、使わざるを得ない環境がいろいろな形で提供できたらよいと考える。

ENGLISH SKILLS　The Power for Professional Success
2015 年 3 月 30 日　第 1 版第 1 刷発行©

編著者　永井　正司
著　者　鈴木　章能　桑村テレサ
　　　　クイン・ケリー　松浦千佳子

発行者　早川征四郎
発行所　開成出版株式会社
　〒101-0052　東京都千代田区神田小川町 3 丁目 26 番 14 号
　TEL.03-5217-0155　FAX.03-5217-0156

ISBN978-4-87603-494-9 C3082